RU
TO THE
WILD WOOD

Tom McCaughren's award-winning novels about the fox have captured the imagination of readers not only in his native Ireland but in many far-flung parts of the world. *Run to the Wild Wood* is the fifth in the series, the others being *Run with the Wind, Run to Earth, Run Swift, Run Free, Run to the Ark and Run for Cover.* All are published by Wolfhound Press, an imprint of Merlin Publishing. A native of Ballymena, Co. Antrim, Tom is a journalist and former broadcaster with RTÉ. He has also written a number of adventure stories for young people and three novels for 'teenagers'. Two of these novels – *In Search of the Liberty Tree* and *Ride a Pale Horse* – are set in the Irish rebellion of 1798. His books have been translated into German, Swedish, Japanese, Korean, French, Dutch, Danish and Latvian.

Also published by Tom McCaughren
From Wolfhound Press

The Fox Series
Book 1 Run with the Wind
Book 2 Run to Earth
Book 3 Run Swift Run Free
Book 4 Run to the Ark
Book 5 Run to the Wild Wood
Book 6 Run for Cover

Tom McCaughren's fox books have won many awards for literature, including: the Reading Association of Ireland Book Award 1985; the Irish Book Awards Medal 1987; the White Ravens selection 1988 (International Youth Library Munich); The Young Persons' Books of the Decade Award 1980–1990 (Irish Children's Book Trust); and the Oscar Wilde Society's Literary Recognition Award 1992.

Contact www.tommccaughren.net for more information or www.merlinwolfhound.com

RUN

TO THE

WILD WOOD

TOM McCAUGHREN

WOLFHOUND PRESS

This paperback edition published in 2007 by
WOLFHOUND PRESS
An Imprint of Merlin Publishing
Newmarket Hall, St Luke's Avenue
Cork Street, Dublin 8, Ireland
Tel: +353 1 4535 866
Fax: +353 1 4535 930
publishing@merlin.ie
www.merlinwolfhound.com

ISBN 0-86327-492-7 Hardback edition 1996
ISBN 0-86327-571-0 First paperback edition 1998
13-Digit ISBN 978-0-86327-944-7 Second paperback edition 2007
10-Digit ISBN 0-86327-944-9

A CIP catalogue record for this book is available from the British Library.

10 9 8 7 6 5 4 3 2 1

Typeset by Carrigboy Typesetting Services
Cover Design by Graham Thew Design
Cover Illustration by William Helps
Printed and bound in J.H. Haynes & Co Ltd, Britain

For all those who asked me to write another fox book

Contents

Author's Note

A few years ago I came into possession of a booklet called *The Fragrant Wood*, a Celtic anthology compiled and edited by Donal Ó Siodhacháin (Irish & Celtic Publications Ltd, Cork, 1990). It was in this booklet that I came across the poem, a verse of which is, quoted in my story . . .

The sweetest bird on the branches singing,
The cuckoo on the top of the green hill;
And death shall never find us
In the bosom of the fragrant wood.

Any reader of early Irish poetry, says Mr. Ó Siodhacháin, will have come across references to the cuckoo. In fact, he tells us, the monks, in particular, seem to have had a phobia about this migratory bird. Again and again, lines of prayer are found begging God, Jesus or some named saint to preserve them from the cuckoo. The monks he explains were praying for the grace to stay on their chosen path and avoid being distracted by things that were not important. The cuckoo on top of the green kill, he says, could be expressed as 'Come with me to the green hill [i.e. the place where eternal things are so abundant that they reach up like an evergreen hill] and there on top you will find the cuckoo [i.e. elusive truth and knowledge] at rest.' I would like to thank Mr. Ó Siodhacháin for his retelling and interpretation of this lovely poem; also Dr John Montague, to whom the booklet is dedicated.

A special word of thanks to John and Kathleen Kelly, of Hollywood, Ballyboughal, Co. Dublin, breeders of Irish wolfhounds, who were kind enough to introduce me and my family to that adorable big animal, and who gave me the opportunity to read *The Irish Wolfhound* by Elizabeth C. Murphy. King John of England, that book tells us, presented an Irish wolfdog to Llewelyn, a Prince of Wales, in about 1210. It goes on to quote W.R. Spencer's poem, *Gelert, Llewelyn's Dog*; it is in that poem that you will find the wolfhound described as 'the flower of all his race, so true, so brave, a lamb at home, a lion in the chase'.

I would also like to acknowledge two other publications: *Irish Proverbs*, compiled by Laurence Flanagan (Gill & Macmillan); and *Even Monkeys Fall from Trees and other Japanese Proverbs*, compiled and translated by David Galef, which my Japanese translator, Masako Okamura, very kindly sent to me.

In one of my earlier fox books, Old Sage Brush says man has no time for the birds, no room for the trees. . . . He might well have added that man has no time for the badgers either. With the destruction of the Fragrant Wood in this story, the badgers are driven from their setts. However, they have lived to tell the tale and seek a new home. In the real world, they might not have been so lucky.

Badgers are still killed officially and unofficially in the Republic of Ireland as the Department of Agriculture believes that they transmit tuberculosis, to cattle. Badgerwatch Ireland disputes this and is trying to convince the department that the culling of badgers should cease. In Britain and Northern Ireland, culling has been discontinued and the British Badger Trust is working hard to try and ensure that it is not reintroduced.

However, relief for the badgers may be on the way. In an experiment funded by the Department of Agriculture, scientists in University College Dublin, have tested the anti-tuberculosis vaccine, BCG, on captive badgers. This is the same vaccine that has been successful in protecting children. The experiment, I'm told, showed that it also protected the badgers against infection, and field trials are expected to begin later this year.

The Minister for Agriculture and Food, Mary Coughlan, said recently that her department was committed to the project to develop a vaccine that would lead to a reduction in what she called, current high level of infection in badgers. It was hoped that, in the longer term, this would reduce the need to cull them. However, she warned that any vaccine would not be available for wider use in the immediate future and the existing strategy (of culling badgers) would remain in place for some time.

Tom McCaughren, 2007

PART ONE

'. . . he found his thoughts dwelling again with much persistence on the solitary grey badger . . . who lived in the middle of the Wild Wood.'

– from *The Wind in the Willows*

ONE

The Year of the Badger

The new moon was cradling the faint outline of the old moon in its lap as the vixen made her way quietly up through the darkened fields. Other creatures of the night who observed her passing noted that she was following a particular path, and was familiar with each and every obstacle, surmounting them with ease and a swish of a brush that was tipped with white. Some, like the owls, who had seen her before, would have known that she was heading for the oak tree on top of the hill.

It was the time of year man called spring, and while he might have noted that the days were getting longer, the vixen and her kind were conscious of the fact that the nights were getting shorter. It was at night that they did most of their hunting as it was always safer to go abroad under cover of darkness. But unlike the owls, the foxes hunted by daylight too, and as the nights grew shorter, they would adjust their eyes and their hunting habits to the dangers of the day.

Trotting up the side of a field, the vixen stopped in her stride, one forepaw suspended, her large black ears twitching to every sound that rose from the valley below. Hearing nothing that posed any danger, her sensitive nose sifted the scents of the night. No danger there either, it told her, so she lifted her nose a little higher and savoured all the things she could read in the wind. Strong scents from a nearby farmyard, a suggestion of pheasant from a clump of ivy-covered trees in a corner of a field, the unmistakable tang of hare moving across the wind. For a moment she was tempted to leave her path and go hunting, but she resisted the urge and continued on up towards the oak tree. Soon the dark outline of the giant tree loomed up against the purple sky, and having paused again to make sure she wasn't being observed, the vixen tip-toed over to the earth she knew was hidden beneath the gnarled roots. Suddenly there was a rustling sound to her right, and she caught a glimpse of a badger shuffling away into the undergrowth. Puzzled, she paused once more and listened. Why, she wondered, should a badger come to a fox earth in the middle of the night? Badgers had their own setts and they were a lot deeper and safer than the cavity under the tree. Before she could come up with an answer, a voice from within told her, 'Don't stand there all night, Vickey. Come in.'

Vickey smiled, and not for the first time wondered how the old fox had known she was there. 'How did you know it was me?' she asked him.

He waited until she had snuggled in beside him. 'Who else but you would come to see an old fox in the middle of the night, instead of taking to the fields to hunt?'

Vickey now became aware of another fox sleeping in one of the many chambers formed by the tangle of roots. He was so small and thin she hadn't noticed him at first. 'How's he getting on?' she inquired.

The old fox snorted to dislodge a small spider that had dropped from one of the roots, and told her, 'He'll be all right.'

'Hop-along and She-la are delighted to have him back,' she went on. 'But they're worried about him. He's failed a lot.'

The old fox offered nothing more by way of reassurance, and after a while Vickey said, 'Sage Brush. I saw a badger on my way in.'

'So?'

'What was it doing here?'

'Who said it was here?'

'Sage Brush,' said Vickey sternly, 'don't play games with me.'

Old Sage Brush smiled. 'All right, so it *was* here.'

'I didn't recognise it – where was it from?'

'Another valley – beyond the hills.'

'And what brought it to the Land of Sinna?' asked Vickey.

'It wanted guidance.'

Realising that the old fox was telling her as little as possible, Vickey asked, 'What sort of guidance? You mean, advice?'

'Something like that.'

'Sage Brush,' said Vickey, her voice becoming stern again, 'what did the badger want?'

The old fox shuffled uncomfortably. 'I told you it wanted guidance.' When Vickey demonstrated her displeasure by remaining silent, he went on. 'They're having a problem.'

'What kind of a problem?'

'They want to move to a new home.'

'And what's that got to do with us?' asked Vickey.

'They can't do it on their own,' said the old fox.

Vickey's heart sank. She had been afraid it might be something like that. 'But Sage Brush . . . ' she said, and for once she found it difficult to put her fears into words. What she wanted to say was that she thought he wasn't really able for things like that any more, that he had earned his place here on the Hill of Old Age, but she was afraid of using the wrong words, afraid she might offend him.

As if reading her mind, he said, 'So you think I'm too old?'

Vickey lowered her head. 'I didn't say that. But you know yourself, your legs are not as strong as they used to be.'

'The legs of a flea are weak,' said the old fox, 'and look how far it can jump.'

'Maybe so,' said Vickey, 'but when it jumps, it's always onto someone else's back.'

'Look at this tree,' said Old Sage Brush. 'It is because it is weak that the wind cannot blow it down. Its weakness is its strength.'

Vickey knew well that the tree had a secret that enabled it to survive. But she also knew that it was the old fox's wisdom, not his legs, that was his strength. However, it was becoming obvious to her that he was in one of his moods, and that she was wasting her time trying to argue with him. So she just said, 'What do you want me to do then? Call a meeting under Beech Paw?'

The old fox shook his head. 'No need. Just pass the road around to a few of our own. Tell them to come and see me up here at the oak.'

Vickey agreed, but as she made her way back down the hill she felt uneasy. Something was nagging at her. In an effort to find out what it was, she found herself going over and over everything the old fox had said. The badgers wanted to move to a new home. They had a problem. Of course they had, otherwise they wouldn't want to move. What was it then? She was at the bottom of the hill when she concluded that it wasn't anything the old fox had said that was making her feel uneasy. It was what he hadn't said. Somehow she had the feeling that he hadn't told her everything. She hopped down into a dry ditch beneath a long line of beeches and crossed an open field towards the quarry where she had her own den. She was still thinking about her conversation with the old fox, and she was still uneasy. The more she thought about it the more she became convinced that the visit of the badger was an event they would all remember. She only hoped it was something they wouldn't regret.

How could she know that what had been discussed under the oak would one day lead the fox world to speak of the Year of the Badger?

TWO

The Year of the Cuckoo

The oak tree where the foxes were to meet was old, very old. It had been struck by lightning more than once, and had died at least twice. Yet still it lived. The ivy which grew up from its roots in a strong single stem could not overpower it. Above where cattle might shelter from the sun and flies, the ivy had wrapped itself around the oak's enormous trunk, then reached for its huge spreading branches. But the tree had flexed its muscles with a strength the ivy could not match, arching its mighty branches upwards and outwards with a power that seemed to burst the choking creeper and take them safely out of reach.

Sweeping over and down almost to the ground, the branches were bare but full of life, insect life that would live and die and feed other forms of life. Over the years some branches, for all their might, had died and broken off, but even they had created new life, the gaping holes from whence they had come offering hiding places for other creatures of the wood. Between the branches where they spread from the trunk, a dense tangle of growth had formed, but no one, not even the foxes, could tell for certain what lived there.

What the foxes did know, and man didn't, was that the ancient oak was hollow, a secret that had saved it from many a storm. While younger, heavier oaks had fallen before the wind, the very same wind had merely caressed the old tree, blowing through it as it would a shell. Finding its way in through the cracks and crevices of time, the wind would leave the same way, and the old fox who lived beneath the gnarled roots would sleep in the sure and certain knowledge that when he awoke, the tree would still be there.

Many of those who saw these things didn't see the tree as anything special. But the old fox, who couldn't see them, saw them in a way that few others could. The years had given him something which, in his own quiet way, he shared with the tree. Not that he was strong – far from it – but it seemed to others that he had an inner strength which, like the oak's, enabled him to survive.

To the little fox who now lay facing him in the shadows beneath the roots of the tree, it seemed that the old fox was forever sleeping. It was a long time since they had shared their thoughts. While man might call it a year, the fox's year is more linked to the seasons, or related to great events. If, therefore, like this young fox, they've been chased by man and his hounds, they will refer to that time as the Year of the Howling Dogs. Or if, like his father, they've managed to outwit a particularly strong hare, they will speak of it as the Year of the Hare. Then again, if they've had an encounter with a stoat, they will tell their young about the Year of the Stoat. In this way, even though the events may have been of relatively short duration, stories of great courage and cunning are handed down from one generation of foxes to another.

The little fox lay with his nose resting on his forepaws. His long black ears, which seemed unusually large in relation to his scrawny body, turned and twitched to every sound in the tree above him. At one stage he extended a timorous forepaw towards his companion, then changed his mind and withdrew it. He was tempted to waken him, not for any particular reason other than to talk to him, but was reluctant to disturb him. However, his youthful fidgeting seemed to communicate itself to the old fox, and without opening his eyes the old fox asked, 'Well, how are you feeling today?'

The little fox shrugged his shoulders. 'All right.'

'You're not eating,' observed the old fox. 'How come?'

'I don't feel like it.'

'But you must eat,' the old fox advised him. 'If you don't eat you won't be able to hunt, and if you can't hunt you won't be able to eat.' The little fox laughed, and promised, 'I will eat – when I'm hungry.'

Before the old fox could argue, another young fox arrived at the entrance to the earth, and sensing the presence of a stranger, paused, his teeth bared in readiness for a fight.

'Take it easy,' said the old fox. 'Don't you recognise your friend?'

The newcomer took a step forward and with a swish of a tail that was tipped with black, peered into the gloom beneath the tangled roots of the oak tree.

'Young Black Tip?' said the little fox, rising to his feet. 'Is that you?'

The other nodded, and hearing the puzzlement in his silence, the old fox told him, 'It's Scat. Your little friend from your cubhood days. Remember how hard you both ran from the howling dogs?'

The Year of the Howling Dogs. Young Black Tip stepped forward. How could he forget? But the Scat he remembered was a hardy little fox, full of vim and vigour – so much so that he recalled how they both had looked at the hills and vowed they were going to find out what lay beyond them.

'I think there are whole new areas over there, just waiting for us to move in,' Young Black Tip had said.

'Places with plenty of food,' Scat had added, 'and plenty of vixens.'

How then could this be Scat – this scrawny little creature, so small and thin his head and ears seemed too big for his body?

'Wait until your eyes get used to the darkness,' said the old fox.

'But Sage Brush,' said Young Black Tip. 'How . . . ?' How could he tell the old fox that had he been able to see, he would have been shocked at the state of their little visitor? Instead, he moved forward and confirming by scent that it was indeed Scat, he bowled his little friend over and in a gentle yet boisterous sham fight they warmly renewed an acquaintance that had been shattered in their flight from the howling dogs.

Gentle though it had been, the reunion with Young Black Tip had exhausted Scat and he was asleep when the others began to arrive.

Whatever about Vickey and Young Black Tip, Old Sage Brush had no difficulty in detecting the footsteps of a fox with three legs. 'Come in, Hop-along,' he said. 'You too, She-la. Make yourselves comfortable.'

Seeing that Scat was asleep, She-la asked, 'How is he?' There wasn't a fox in the valley who hadn't rejoiced with She-la and Hop-along when their cub had returned from beyond the hills, for it is the nature of things in the fox world that few if any ever come back to the place of their birth. As Old Sage Brush had put it, 'the falling blossom never returns to the branch'. However, their rejoicing was mixed with concern when they saw that the little fox hadn't flourished and matured in a way that most foxes do when they strike out on their own. But then all were mindful of the fact that Scat and his brother Scab, who had suffered from the itch, had always been puny. It was a failing which, rightly or wrongly, they put down to the fact that the father of the cubs had lost a leg in one of man's traps and had been unable to hunt as well as he might have wished when the cubs needed something more substantial than milk.

Sensing She-la's concern, the old fox assured her, 'He's just resting. Young Black Tip and himself were having a bit of fun and he's tired out.'

As they settled themselves down on the bare earth, which had been flattened and smoothed by the furry bodies of many foxes, Old Sage Brush asked, 'Well, Hop-along, how are things over in the blackthorns?'

'Fine,' came the reply. 'The bushes are full of birds and the fields are full of rabbits.'

'The sleeping sickness seems to have gone,' She-la told him. 'I've never seen so many rabbits.'

Old Sage Brush nodded. 'So I hear. Young Black Tip brought me one.'

Young Black Tip sat up and looked at him. He had brought one all right, but he had just left it for him in the undergrowth nearby and hadn't mentioned it.

'It smells good,' the old fox told him.

Young Black Tip smiled. Unlike Scat, he had mated and had been out hunting for his vixen who was now suckling cubs. Catching an extra rabbit for the old fox had been no trouble, there had been so many of them. He had also left one over in the blackthorns where Hop-along would find it, but he didn't want to offend Hop-along by letting him know where it had come from. 'Ah, here's Little Running Fox,' he said, changing the subject. He greeted his sister, then stepped aside as other foxes began to arrive: a young fox with a white star on her forehead called Twinkle, her parents, Sinnéad and Skulking Dog, his own parents, Vickey and Black Tip, and then one who, as always, preferred to lie outside.

'Ratwiddle!' said the old fox. 'Come in.'

No one was surprised, or indeed disappointed, when Ratwiddle ignored the old fox and, lying down just within earshot of the earth, began to scratch himself.

'Now,' said Vickey, addressing the old fox, 'if you want to know how far a flea can jump, you just might find out.'

Old Sage Brush smiled. 'It's not what's in Ratwiddle's fur I'm interested in. It's what's in his mind.'

There was a time when the younger foxes would have sniggered at such a remark. But not any more. Once, when they had been trying to catch minnows in the river, Ratwiddle had told them, 'If you don't look up you won't see the water.' They had only been cubs then and had laughed as he had trotted off, head cocked stiffly to one side as usual. It was only when they too had looked up that they had seen a wall of water bearing down on them from the dam. They had been lucky they hadn't drowned. That was how they had become aware that Ratwiddle possessed an uncanny knack of knowing things that were going to happen. He wasn't always able to express what he knew in terms others could understand, but he was always right.

For the moment, however, Ratwiddle's mind didn't appear to be focused on either the future or the present. While the stiffness of his neck meant that he always had one eye on the sky and, it seemed to many, on the future, he was vigorously engaged in trying to dislodge his fleas, an activity which made the others shuffle farther back into the earth. Having had a good scratch, he lay down and closed his eyes, and they reckoned he was thinking of nothing more important than the rats he had been hunting down by the lake. Leaving him to roam in the pathways of his mind, they turned their attention to Old Sage Brush.

'What we want to know,' said Black Tip, 'is what's on *your* mind.'

'Well,' said the old fox, and he changed his position to relieve the ache in his bones, 'as Vickey has no doubt told you, I had a visitor, a badger.'

Hop-along, who was licking the stump of his leg where his paw used to be, stopped and asked, 'What did it want?'

'It was a boar badger,' the old fox told him, 'and it brought a message from a place they call the Fragrant Wood.'

'Sounds lovely,' said Hop-along's mate, She-la.

Old Sage Brush, who often savoured the scent of pine from the woods beyond the oak, nodded. 'I can just imagine it. But it seems a great tragedy has befallen them.'

'Why, what happened?' asked Skulking Dog.

'My visitor didn't say exactly,' the old fox informed him. 'But they need our help.'

'You told me all they needed was guidance,' Vickey reminded him.

The old fox nodded.

'It's strange,' said Skulking Dog. 'I mean, badgers usually keep to themselves. And they don't particularly like foxes.'

'You can say that again,' said Hop-along. 'Once, when I was out hunting with Fang – do you remember Fang?' The older foxes nodded, and he went on. 'We had a run-in with a badger. Fang was a very strong fox, but he came off worst.'

Vickey smiled. She remembered Fang well, for he had fought with Black Tip to see which one of them should have her as a mate. Black Tip had won, but it had been a close thing.

'Fang went into a badger sett to see if there were any rabbits in it,' Hop-along continued. 'The next thing I knew he came sailing back out of it. He had met a badger and it wasn't too pleased to see him.'

'Maybe,' suggested the old fox, 'it didn't see him. If it kicked him out, it was probably with its hind feet.'

'Anyway,' said Sinnéad, 'badgers can't see very well.'

'And their hearing isn't much better,' added Twinkle.

Usually at such meetings, the younger foxes didn't speak until they were spoken to, but since Twinkle was Sinnéad's daughter, and Sinnéad was the old fox's daughter, no one seemed to mind, especially as old fox added, 'Precisely.'

Black Tip smiled. 'So they come to a blind fox for guidance!'

Old Sage Brush grunted. Black Tip had often acted as his eyes and, he knew, was paying him a compliment.

'Is that all there is to it then?' asked Vickey. 'They just want us to guide them to a new sett?'

'What else?' asked the old fox.

'How many of us will it take to do it?' asked Skulking Dog.

'Just a few.'

'All right,' said Vickey. 'We'll do it. Black Tip and myself!'

Sinnead stood up beside her mate, Skulking Dog, and announced, 'We'll go too. That should be enough.'

'No need,' replied the old fox. 'I've given the matter some thought and I've come to the conclusion that this is a job for the younger foxes.'

Vickey heaved a sigh of relief. She had been hoping that the old fox wouldn't propose going himself.

'Maybe Little Running Fox, Twinkle, and Scat,' the old fox went on.

'But Scat's not well,' said She-la. 'Hop-along and I are very concerned about him.'

'Don't worry, he'll have plenty of time to build up his strength,' the old fox assured her. 'Anyway, I was going to suggest that you and Hop-along might come along with us.'

Vickey sat up with a start. 'You mean you're going too?'

The old fox nodded.

'But why?' asked Sinnéad. 'Why not let the strongest do it?'

Knowing that what the vixens were really asking was why he had chosen the youngest and weakest, the old fox answered as he often did, with another question. 'What is strength? I want a fox who is slow and sure-footed. That is why I choose Hop-along. I want a fox who is small and fast, that is why I choose Scat. Who better to find the paths we must travel than Little Running Fox, and what brighter star to guide me than Twinkle?'

'But who will guide them?' asked Skulking Dog.

'I will,' said the old fox. 'Don't worry. The badgers have told me all I need to know.'

The older foxes were perplexed, but they knew there was no point in arguing. The old fox, they could see, had given the matter a lot of thought. He had not chosen Young Black Tip because he had a mate and cubs to look after. The other young foxes had no such ties, none of them having mated.

'You said Scat would have plenty of time to get his strength back,' said She-la. 'When do you propose to go?'

'When the cuckoo comes,' the old fox told her. 'Wait until you hear its call. Then it will be time to go.'

Vickey slipped out of the earth and lay as close to Ratwiddle as she dared. 'Ratwiddle,' she whispered. 'Ratwiddle!' When he opened his eyes, she asked, 'Did you hear what Old Sage Brush said?'

'All I can hear,' he told her, 'is the singing inside my head.'

'Singing?' asked Vickey. 'What singing?'

'Man,' he said, as if in a dream. 'Man is singing.'

Having heard man's voice as he hunted the fox and dug for the badger, Vickey said, 'If man sings, it must be like a crow.'

'No,' answered Ratwiddle. 'The voices are softer. More like the cuckoo.'

'And where is he?' prompted Vickey, desperate to discover what dangers Ratwiddle might be seeing.

'He's standing on an eel,' said Ratwiddle, 'and he's singing like a cuckoo.'

Convinced that the rats he ate must surely have addled Ratwiddle's brain, Vickey joined Black Tip, who was now leaving, and together they made their way back down the hill.

THREE

The Year of the Owl

Bluebells had blossomed everywhere, giving a distinctly bluish tint to the valley the foxes called the Land of Sinna. As Old Sage Brush followed Scat through the woods, he could feel the soft stems giving way before his forelegs and squelching slightly beneath his paws. It had been a long time since he had seen bluebells, or indeed any flowers, and as he tried to remember what they were like it occurred to him that man and his dogs had deprived him of more than his family when they had dug him out of his earth. The probing sticks had blinded him, but he had lived and found a reason for living in his one surviving cub, Sinnéad. She had mated with Skulking Dog, and now they had Twinkle, who bore her mother's little white star on her forehead. Twinkle had grown into a lovely young fox, he thought. Eventually she would have cubs of her own, but in the meantime spring was at its height and already the sounds of new life were everywhere.

'Tell me, Scat,' said the old fox. 'What's it like?'

'What's what like?' asked the little fox.

'What you see. Look around you and tell me.'

'Well, I'm looking for cuckoo spit,' the little fox told him, 'but I can't see any.'

'And why are you looking for that?'

'So that I'll know when the cuckoo has come.'

Old Sage Brush stopped and lay down among the bluebells to rest. 'Sure cuckoo spit has nothing to do with cuckoos. If you have a close look at it you'll find it's just the nest of a small insect. Now tell me, what do you see?'

'The wood is blue,' Scat told him. 'There are bluebells everywhere, and primroses in the ditches. The grass is getting longer and it shines when it bends before the breeze. The bushes and trees are sprouting new leaves, and the birds are flitting in and out of the hedgerows. The gorse is in full bloom – you'd think it was on fire – and there are white flowers on the blackthorn'

'That's nice,' said the old fox, and cocking his ears this way and that, he matched the sound of the birds and the breeze to the images that Scat had conjured up in his mind. Bright blue as far as his inner eye could see, the quiet yellow of the primrose, the blazing gold of the gorse.

'But I don't see any white bluebells,' Scat added. 'Are you sure there is such a thing?'

'Of course there is,' the old fox assured him. 'Now lead on and let your nose tell you where they are.'

What Scat found at the edge of the wood was what man in the locality mistakenly called wild garlic. If the little fox had taken a closer look at it, he would have found that unlike the bluebell, it had a triangular stem, for it was in fact a plant called three-cornered leek. An escapee from a garden, it had spread along hedgerows in the area and some people used it to give a garlic flavour to their food. Farmers, however, strove to keep their cows from eating it, as it gave an equally strong but much less welcome flavour to their milk

'What do you want me to do with it?' asked Scat.

'Eat it,' said the old fox.

'But I'm not hungry,' protested Scat.

'You will be if you eat the white bluebell,' the old fox assured him. 'And you must eat. I told your mother I would build you up before the cuckoo comes.'

Dutifully, Scat settled himself among the white flowers and began to chew them. Immediately a strong aroma of garlic began to rise from them, and moving upwind, Old Sage Brush lay down in the shade of the nearby trees.

As word of what Old Sage Brush proposed to do spread throughout the valley, the fox population talked of little else. Dog foxes out hunting stopped to discuss it with other foxes, and when they brought food back to their earths, they would lie outside and relate the latest news to the vixens inside. As the vixens were suckling their cubs, they couldn't hunt for themselves and the entrance to the earths was as far as the dogs were allowed to go. Likewise, vixens who hadn't mated, but were acting as 'aunts' for the newborn cubs, brought titbits of news as well as titbits of food.

Those who didn't know Old Sage Brush as well as they might, thought the idea of helping the badgers was the foolish notion of a fox who was long past his prime, and those who had seen the state of Scat agreed. Perhaps the only ones who thought it was a good idea were Young Black Tip, Little Running Fox and Twinkle. But then they were young and it was the old fox who had shown them the ways of the wild. Whether Scat thought it was a good idea, no one knew, for they suddenly discovered that he had developed a dreadful breath, so dreadful in fact that it dulled their sense of smell! Even his parents, who were anxious that he should eat, were mystified as to why he was eating white bluebells and were so overcome by the smell of garlic that they couldn't bring themselves to ask.

For his part, Scat was puzzled by the fact that no one seemed to want to talk to him any more. Whenever he arrived at the entrance to an earth, the occupants made an excuse and left by the back. Even his best friends were avoiding him. Yet only a short time ago, they had shared their earths and their food with him. Not that he had eaten much, but now he was being denied not only companionship but the merest sustenance by those he had considered his friends.

'It's not fair,' he said at last.

Like everyone else, Old Sage Brush was making Scat keep his distance, and the little fox was lying in the grass beside the ancient oak tree.

'What's wrong with you now?' asked the old fox, who was dozing in the earth below.

'Nothing.' There was silence from the earth, and a few moments later Scat said, 'Sage Brush.'

'What?'

'Do you not get lonely, living here alone?'

'Alone?' The old fox snorted. 'I'm never alone. The tree above me is full of life, or haven't you noticed?'

'But surely it's not the kind of life that keeps you company,' argued the little fox.

Old Sage Brush came out and lay down as near Scat as he dared. 'Scat,' he said, 'you have a lot to learn. In the hollow recesses of this tree live birds and bats. Their droppings give life to the tree, the tree gives life to them, and together they give life to me.'

'I don't understand,' said Scat.

'It's very simple,' the old fox continued. 'When I hear a twig fall, I know it is daylight and the rook is building its nest. When the bat flutters from its perch, I know it is dusk and the insects that live in the tree are on the wing. When the owl takes to the wing, I know by the way it screeches that it is almost dark and time to hunt.'

'But how can you hunt?' asked Scat. 'When you cannot see?'

Old Sage Brush smiled. Scat, he suspected, was at last beginning to think of his own stomach. 'When darkness falls,' the old fox explained, 'I can see as well as anyone else. The screech of the owl forces the creatures of the night to move and, like the owl, my ears tell me where to find them. But then, of course, my friends sometimes leave me a nice juicy rabbit, and I don't have to hunt to eat.'

Scat sighed. 'Sage Brush,' he said. 'I think the owl is screeching now.'

'Good,' said the old fox, and even though he knew it was daylight, told him, 'Let's hunt, then.'

As they trotted through the woods once again, Old Sage Brush said, 'Well, Scat, what did you see today?'

'Nothing,' came the reply.

'How can you see nothing?' said the old fox. 'Unless you're walking around with your eyes closed.'

'Well, I didn't see much, except two snails nosing.'

'How do you mean, nosing?'

The little fox shrugged. 'They were in their shells, but they seemed to be nosing – you know, like cows.'

'And how many did you see?' asked the old fox.

'Two. They were in under a bush. Then I saw two more in the long grass. They were doing the same.'

'Did you eat them?'

'Of course not. I told you – they were in their shells.'

'Just as well,' grunted the old fox.

'Why?'

The old fox sighed. 'Did your parents never teach you anything?'

'Of course they did. But it was you who showed us the ways of the wild, remember?'

The old fox nodded. 'So I did.'

They trotted on, and having considered how he might say what he wanted to say without offending his young companion, the old fox said, 'Tell me, Scat. If the snail, which is so slow, can find a mate, why can't a fleet-footed young fox like yourself find one?'

'Oh.' Scat stopped in his tracks. 'Is that what they were doing?'

'Well?' asked the old fox. 'You didn't find a vixen when you took to the hills, did you?'

'There were plenty of vixens, all right,' Scat replied. 'But there were plenty of dog foxes too. And they were all a lot bigger than I was. Stronger too. When it came to a fight I hadn't a hope.'

'Ah, so that was the problem.' In the field where the white bluebells grew, several rabbits bounded towards their burrows in the nearest ditch. One delayed, and with a rare turn of speed, Scat got to the burrow before it. Unaware that he had got his appetite back, the little fox carried his catch back to the oak tree. Old Sage Brush smiled, and followed.

'You know,' said Scat, as he munched at the rabbit, 'I've never even seen a cuckoo.'

'Well, you know something, Scat,' the old fox confessed, 'I've never seen one either.'

Scat stopped eating. 'But how could you, when you're blind?'

'True, but I wasn't always blind.'

Seeing how the old fox was enjoying the rabbit too, Scat asked, 'Do you think I'll be ready? I mean, by the time the cuckoo calls?'

'All you have to do is build up your strength,' the old fox told him. 'Before you know it, you'll be fit to fight a dragon.'

Scat laughed. As a cub he had often heard the older foxes tell stories about other animals that had once lived in the valleys – huge animals with long necks and tails and scaly backs – and strange birds that had flown over them – big birds, with teeth in their beaks and claws on their feet, that could pluck a sheep or a fox from the fields and tear it to pieces. Some of the stories even spoke of monsters with breaths of fire. Dragons, they were called, but even cubs knew there was no such thing.

Scat finished eating. 'I couldn't fight a dragon*fly* if it landed on my nose this minute.'

The old fox smiled. 'What would you say if I told you that the place where the badgers want us to take them is known to them as the Valley of the Dragon?'

Thinking that Old Sage Brush was joking, Scat laughed again, only to find that the old fox was no longer smiling.

* * *

While Young Black Tip understood why Old Sage Brush had not asked him to go along with them, he was deeply disappointed. True, he had a vixen and cubs now, but the cubs were still suckling and he would play no part in their upbringing until such time as they were weaned and needed to know the ways of the wild. For the moment his only function was to bring food to the earth for his mate.

When, a short time after the meeting with Old Sage Brush, Young Black Tip spoke to his parents and expressed his disappointment at not being chosen, they understood, and said that if he wanted to go they would hunt for his mate until he returned. They too were disappointed that they hadn't been chosen, for they were anxious that the old fox should have as much support as possible. Young Black Tip, they knew, would be a great strength to him and indeed to the others.

'Perhaps,' suggested Vickey, when she went to see Old Sage Brush, 'he could hunt for you.'

The old fox smiled. 'Now there's an idea.'

Vickey was pleased, but even with the addition of Young Black Tip she was far from happy. She still felt the old fox hadn't told her everything. Yet, even when Young Black Tip and Little Running Fox asked her to repeat the stories she had once told them about monsters and dragons, she didn't suspect that they were preparing themselves for the journey that lay ahead of them.

FOUR

The Year of the Tiger

A flurry of seeds rose into the air from a field of dandelion clocks, then floated gently back to earth. The owl in the old oak tree opened her eyes and, seeing it was only foxes crossing the field, settled back down on her eggs.

Nesting time for some smaller birds had also come to the Land of Sinna, and so had the cuckoo. Had man seen the foxes crossing the fields, he might have wondered where they were going. Then again he might not. They were after all in what he called Glensinna. It was, he knew, a name that had come from the Gaelic and meant 'the Valley of the Fox'.

Had Old Sage Brush seen the shower of white seeds rising from the field, he would have advised caution in case the seeds might betray their presence. However, the seeds were too delicate for even his sensitive nose to feel, and he was unaware of them. All he was aware of, as he trotted along beside Twinkle, was the lilting call of the cuckoo spreading across the countryside as softly as summer itself.

There were others besides the owl who also watched from the edge of the wood. Vickey and her friends did not know what dangers the journey might hold for Old Sage Brush and his companions, but they feared the worst. One, whose eye was always cocked to the sky, watched the seeds they had disturbed fall back to earth, but if he knew what lay ahead of them, he wasn't telling. When, without warning, he seemed to lose interest, and ran off in his usual erratic fashion, the others took no notice. His mind, they knew, was on things no ordinary foxes could fathom. Theirs were on an old fox who was stubborn and blind, another who had only three legs, and several who were too young to know any better.

The young foxes, however, were full of the joys of life. The sun was shining and their spirits were high. Racing ahead, Little Running Fox paused on one hill, then another, picking out the markers the badgers had told the old fox to follow. Close on the heels of Twinkle and Old Sage Brush came Hop-along and She-la, and following them was their young dog, Scat.

In the time he had spent at the oak tree waiting to hear the cuckoo call, Scat had improved a lot. Thanks to Old Sage Brush, his appetite had returned. Whether this was due to the white bluebells purging his stomach, or the old fox purging his mind, none of the other foxes could tell. The important thing was that he was eating again, and while it was generally accepted that he would always be small and scrawny, he was slowly but surely regaining his strength. In bringing up the rear, his job was to make sure no danger came upon them from behind. This meant a lot of running, a lot of looking and very little time for hunting. It also meant there was little or no time for talking, at least when they were on the move, and Scat was always glad when Young Black Tip sought him out.

Hunting for the others kept Young Black Tip busy, but he was enjoying it. As they moved into new areas, he found the rabbits as healthy and plentiful as they were in the Land of Sinna. Occasionally he also came upon a pheasant, but it was above all a time when birds of every kind were laying, and sometimes when there was nothing left to lick but bones, he would hunt around for eggs. The old fox, he knew, was particularly fond of eggs, for he never stopped until he had licked the shells clean.

It was during one of Young Black Tip's visits that Scat asked, 'Did you ever get the feeling something's watching you?'

Young Black Tip jerked up his head so that he could see above the grass and looked anxiously around. 'You mean someone's following us?'

Scat shrugged. 'Not so much following us. But you know when something's watching you, you can sort of feel it.'

'The only thing I've seen are fox tracks,' said Young Black Tip. 'Have you seen anything?'

'No,' Scat told him. 'It's just a feeling I get sometimes.'

Young Black Tip was silent. 'You remember,' he said after a moment's reflection, 'when we were going to Old Sage Brush to get him to show us the ways of the wild?'

Scat nodded, and Young Black Tip went on, 'We didn't know it then, but our parents were keeping an eye on us. I don't suppose some of them could be doing the same again?'

Scat shook his head. 'We're a lot older now. Sure it's me that's keeping an eye on my parents now. And you're a parent yourself.'

Young Black Tip nodded. They had long since struck out on their own all right, and their parents wouldn't feel any need to look after them. 'Unless they're worried about Old Sage Brush and Hop-along.'

'I suppose they're worried about them all right,' said Scat, 'but they know we can look after them.'

Young Black Tip raised his head and looked around again. 'You don't suppose it's man, do you?'

Scat snorted to show his contempt. 'If it was man we would have heard him long ago. Or seen his tracks. No, what I felt was silent. I got the strange feeling it was watching us, and it left no tracks.' When his friend didn't reply, he asked, 'Do you think we should tell Old Sage Brush?'

Young Black Tip shook his head. 'No need to worry him. Or Hop-along. At least not yet. Just keep your eyes skinned and I'll do the same.'

They got up to go, and Scat added, 'We'd need to let Little Running Fox know. And Twinkle, when you get a chance.'

Young Black Tip nodded. 'Right. And take care. If there *is* something out there we'll have to tread carefully until we find out what it is.'

They parted, Scat saying, 'Until tonight then.'

It was the old fox who had decreed that they should travel by day. As cubbing time came and went, the nights were getting shorter. Better, he thought, that they should travel by day, when they would have more time to rest and Little Running Fox could more easily find the markers that would chart their path.

Having been alerted by Young Black Tip that something might be watching them, Little Running Fox and Twinkle were extra vigilant, but they saw nothing either, and that night as they settled into a disused earth they wondered if, perhaps, it had been Scat's imagination.

While the days were getting warmer the nights were still cold, and when they snuggled into one another they were glad of the warmth. It also minded the young foxes of the nights they had been warm and snug in their own earths, listening to their mothers telling them stories. Now as they listened to the older foxes, they found that She-la and Hop-along were just as puzzled as they were about their ultimate destination.

'We all know,' said Hop-along, 'that there's no such thing as a dragon.'

'It's not so long ago,' Old Sage Brush reminded him, 'that you would have said there's no such thing as a monster. And what is a dragon, but a monster that breathes fire?'

'You mean, our visit to man's place?' asked She-la.

'Exactly,' said the old fox. 'Remember what we found when cloud obscured the Great Running Fox in the Sky and we took a wrong turn?'

Hop-along nodded. 'The Land of the Giant Ginger Cats.'

It was a story the young foxes had heard before, but one they never tired of hearing, and they snuggled in closer to each other as Hop-along and She-la recounted some of the strange things they had seen.

It had happened when the weather had closed in and they could no longer see the Great Running Fox in the Sky. During their first winter, the younger foxes had watched the Great Running Fox come down to touch the hills, and had used it as a marker when they had gone out to hunt, just as they had been taught to do. They couldn't know that man had once used the same configuration of stars for guidance on his travels, although he had named it after the implement he used to till the fields. It wouldn't have occurred to man that the stars he called the Plough were also in the shape of a running fox, with the last three stars forming a tail, but that was the way the foxes saw it.

'Without the Great Running Fox to guide us,' She-la recalled, 'we lost our way.'

'That was when we met Scavenger,' Hop-along continued. 'He was a great little fox. Scrawny, like Scat here, but fearless.'

'And is it really true that you raided the duck pond in the Land of the Giant Ginger Cats?' asked Scat.

'Of course we did,' said She-la. 'You were there too – all of you, for it was only a short time before you were born.'

'And tell us again,' urged Twinkle, 'what did you see?'

'We saw mice,' She-la told them. 'Giant mice that carried their young in pouches on their bellies.' She lowered her voice and continued, 'We saw birds that were as big as horses, and horses with humps.'

'It's true,' vouched Hop-along. 'There were creatures that had necks so long they could eat leaves from the tree-tops without even stretching. And there were some with noses so long they could eat off the ground without even bending.'

'And don't forget the cats,' Old Sage Brush reminded him.

'That's right,' Hop-along went on. 'The cats were bigger than anything you've ever seen. Giants, they were.'

'Were they big enough to catch the giant mice?' asked Young Black Tip.

'They were of course,' said She-la. 'But it was a sort of farm. They were all in pens, and when they roared for food man came and fed them.'

'Did any of them breathe fire like a dragon?' asked Twinkle.

'No,' the old fox told her. 'But from what the others told me the giant cats were the colour of fire.'

'Their fur was like the flames of the field,' Hop-along confirmed.

'Of course,' added Old Sage Brush, 'I couldn't see them. But I could hear them growling, and it's something I wouldn't wish to hear again.'

'I saw an animal once that breathed fire,' said Young Black Tip.

Scat sat up. 'Where?'

'Up at the old oak tree. It had just been eating white bluebells.'

'Very funny,' Scat retorted, and jumping on his friend, wrestled him all around the floor of the earth until She-la made them behave themselves.

The old fox smiled to himself and drifted off to sleep. Soon Hop-along and She-la were asleep too, and moving out to the entrance, the young foxes lay down and talked. It was a cool, clear night, and the countryside was bathed in that soft light of the moon that they had come to know as gloomglow.

'I'm still getting the feeling something is watching us,' whispered Scat.

'What, you mean now?' asked Young Black Tip.

'When we're on the move,' said Scat. 'I get the feeling something's following us.'

'But if there *is* something out there,' whispered Little Running Fox, 'how come it hasn't left any tracks?'

The crack of a twig nearby made them all sit up with a start. Visions of giant mice and giant ginger cats came flooding into their minds, and when, a few moments later, something large came plodding through the undergrowth towards them, they all turned tail and dived back into the earth.

'What was that?' panted Twinkle.

'I don't know,' said Young Black Tip.

'Listen,' said Scat. 'It's still there.'

Trying not to breathe too loudly, in case they might be heard, they turned their sensitive ears this way and that, and knew that whatever giant animal had come upon them in the dark was still there. They could hear it breathing, and knew its large mouth was down close to the entrance to the earth, sniffing, wondering what was inside. Fearful of what it might be, but comforted by the knowledge that it was too big to come in after them, they retreated to the inner chamber where the older foxes were sleeping and snuggled in close beside them.

Daylight came and, as always, Old Sage Brush advised the younger foxes to proceed with care. Fearful of what they had heard during the night, yet curious to know what it was, they had crept up to the front entrance to peep out. 'Don't forget what I told you,' said the old fox. 'Vary your path. And if you enter an earth by the front, leave it by the back.' For once the younger foxes were glad to accept his advice, for they had seen that something big and heavy had trampled the scrub around the entrance to the earth.

Convinced that there must be an explanation for what was happening, Young Black Tip went much further than he normally would in his search for food that day. Moving in a wide sweep around the others, he scanned the fields with his eyes and his nose. He even went back to the earth, but by that time the cows had obliterated any other tracks that might have been there. Elsewhere he found a variety of tracks, some old, some new, but the only unusual tracks he came across were those of another fox. They were unusual in that they seemed to wander all over the place, and he wasn't surprised when, a short time later, he came across the fox that had made them.

'Ratwiddle!' he said. 'What are *you* doing here?'

Ratwiddle was lying in the long grass scratching himself. As always, his head was twisted upwards and sideways so that he looked with one eye at the sky. 'Here?' he replied. 'Where is here? All I can see is there.

'But what are you doing following us?' asked Young Black Tip.

'I follow only what I see in my mind,' said Ratwiddle.

Knowing that his mother hadn't been able to get much sense out of Ratwiddle, Young Black Tip said, 'Vickey told us you saw man standing on an eel, and that he was singing like a cuckoo. What else do you see?'

Ratwiddle scratched himself even more vigorously, and Young Black Tip jumped back in case he might get some of his fleas.

'Please, Ratwiddle,' he pleaded. 'What else do you see?'

Ratwiddle stopped scratching. 'I see foxes running from the wolf. I see hares running with the flowers. I see flames running to the sky.'

'Do you see any dragons?' asked Young Black Tip.

'My mind is full of dragons,' answered Ratwiddle. Speaking as if in a dream, he added, 'You can't kill dragons, you know.'

Before Young Black Tip could ask Ratwiddle to come back with him, Ratwiddle got up, trotted away across the field at a crazy angle and disappeared through a hedge. At least, the young fox told himself, he would be able to tell his friends who had been watching them. But then, he wondered, how could it have been Ratwiddle? He always had one eye on the ground and one on the sky.

FIVE

The Year of the Goat

Old Sage Brush was surprised to hear that Ratwiddle had followed them. 'It's the first time he's ever done that,' said the old fox. 'I wonder what's on his mind.'

Young Black Tip looked at the ground, saying, 'Dragons.'

Hop-along laughed. 'Dragons?'

'I asked him if he could see any dragons,' Young Black Tip explained, 'and he said his mind was full of dragons.'

'That's about the only sensible thing I've ever heard him say,' remarked She-la.

'Perhaps the only thing we could make sense of,' said the old fox. 'The problem is, there's usually a grain of sense in everything he says, if only we could understand it.'

'But hares running with flowers?' said She-la. 'And wolves? There are no wolves nowadays. Not even in the Land of the Giant Ginger Cats.'

'What was it he said again?' asked Hop-along.

'He said he could see the fox running from the wolf,' Young Black Tip reminded him.

Hop-along shifted uncomfortably, and seeing her mate was thinking he wouldn't be able to run very far,

She-la assured him, 'Ratwiddle's for the birds.' She turned to Old Sage Brush. 'Maybe we should bring him in – before he brings any trouble upon us.'

'We could try,' said the old fox, 'but how do you bring someone back to the present, when his mind is somewhere in the future?'

Having travelled a good distance, they were resting on the side of a hill, enjoying the warmth of a sun that was shining from a fluffy sky.

'There's an abandoned badger sett down there among the bushes,' said Little Running Fox. 'If you three could wait there, we could go out and try and find him.'

'Good idea,' said She-la. 'He's a danger to himself as much as to anybody else.'

Old Sage Brush pushed himself up. 'All right, if it'll make you happy.'

Hop-along hobbled after him, and when She-la turned around to signal that the two of them were safely underground, the young foxes sped off in search of Ratwiddle. Splitting up, they hurried through the fields, stopping now and then to look, or listen, or sniff a scent. But of Ratwiddle there was no sign, and eventually they returned to a pre-arranged spot. Ratwiddle, they realised, might be for the birds, but he was just as difficult to catch.

'All I saw was a dead cow,' Little Running Fox reported.

'Where was that?' asked Young Black Tip.

'There's a farm just over the hill. It was lying in one of the fields.'

'Were there any lambs?' asked Twinkle.

Little Running Fox nodded. 'Some of the fields were full of them.'

'What do you think?' asked Scat.

'Ratwiddle wouldn't go near them, would he?'

'He's only interested in rats,' said Young Black Tip. 'But if he wanders in his own crazy way through a field of lambs, he'll get shot.'

Realising that they had no time to lose, the others followed Little Running Fox up over the hill. Some of the lambs, they could see, had just been born, and they knew they were running a great risk themselves in going so near them.

'The dead cow's in that field over there,' Little Running Fox told them.

Taking care not to be seen, they made their way up along the hedgerow, but when they looked out to where the cow had been, all they could see were marks on the grass, showing clearly that something had dragged it away across the field.

'There it is, over there,' whispered Little Running Fox, and as their eyes followed the drag marks, they were just in time to see the hindquarters of the cow, its legs stiff as sticks, being pulled through a gap in a hedge.

Retreating to the safety of the nearby hill, the young foxes made their way in under a clump of gorse.

Did you see that?' said Scat. 'It looked as if it had been killed by a giant ginger cat.

'Or a wolf,' said Twinkle. 'And it was pulling it into its lair.'

'Don't be silly,' said Young Black Tip. 'There are no wolves any more. And there are no giant ginger cats, at least not around here.'

'Then what was Ratwiddle talking about?' asked Scat. 'He said the fox would run from the wolf.'

Young Black Tip shook his head. 'I don't know. I doubt if he knows himself. But there must be some other explanation for what we saw.

'If Ratwiddle is over at that farm,' said Little Running Fox, 'he'll be running all right, but it won't be from a wolf.

'If you're so sure,' said Scat, 'why don't you go over there and look for him yourself?'

Little Running Fox got to her feet. 'I will too,' she said indignantly.

'No,' said Young Black Tip. 'I'll go.' His sister protested, but he was adamant. 'Where there are sheep there are sheepdogs. And if they come after me, or Ratwiddle, the three of you can draw them off. You've all got a good turn of speed.'

Before they could argue, he was gone. Hurrying, in case they might miss anything, they followed him as far as the nearest hedge. There they lay down and watched him approach the spot where the cow had been dragged through the gap. He paused, then bravely trotted through. They held their breath, but whatever they were expecting, it didn't prepare them for what happened next. Without warning, Young Black Tip came sailing back out through the gap. He landed with a thump, and picking himself up, raced back up the hill with all the speed of a scalded cat. Breaking cover, the other three rushed forward to meet him, anxious to know what had happened.

However, Young Black Tip refused to answer any of their questions. 'It's time we were getting back,' was all he said, and, wide-eyed with wonder, they galloped after him.

There was a stranger at the sett when they returned. He was a big strong fox, probably a season older than either Hop-along or She-la, but with fangs that suggested he was a fierce fighter.

'This is Fang,' said Hop-along. 'Remember, I told you about him when we met under the old oak?' The young foxes nodded. They had heard a lot about Fang – and how good a fighter he was.

Noting that one of them had a dark tip on his tail instead of the usual white one, Fang said, 'And you must be related to Black Tip?'

Young Black Tip nodded and attempted to sit down so that he could swirl his tail around for all to see. But he felt a great soreness in his hindquarters and quickly changed his mind. 'Black Tip and Vickey,' he replied. 'They're my parents.'

'Ah, Vickey,' sighed Fang. 'How is she?'

Young Black Tip shrugged. For some reason he felt embarrassed that a stranger should be asking after his mother. Perhaps, he thought, it was because he had heard the other fox had fought for Vickey, and might, if the fight had turned out differently, have been his father. 'I don't know,' he mumbled. 'All right, I suppose.'

Sensing his embarrassment, Old Sage Brush told Fang, 'You can take it from me, she's as beautiful as ever.'

Fang smiled. The old fox might be blind, but he sensed many things, and beauty in its various forms was one of them.

'This is their daughter, Little Running Fox,' said Hop-along, continuing with the introductions. 'Twinkle is Sinnéad's daughter, and this little fellow here, his name's Scat. He's ours.'

'And, of course,' said She-la, nodding towards a fox who was lying a little distance away, 'you would have known Ratwiddle.'

Surprised, the young foxes turned to see Ratwiddle, scratching himself as usual and apparently completely unaware that they had been looking everywhere for him.

'You did well to bring him in,' said the old fox.

Not knowing what to say, the young foxes said nothing. Instead, Scat turned to Fang and asked, 'Have you been following us, by any chance?'

Fang smiled. 'What makes you think that?'

'It's just that sometimes I felt as if something was watching us.'

'That's very sharp of you,' said Fang. 'As a matter of fact, I *was* watching you. I was wondering what you were up to.'

When Old Sage Brush explained the purpose of their journey, Fang said, 'Well, I really came in to warn you. You're on a farm where man doesn't like foxes or badgers.'

'How do you mean?' asked She-la.

'From what I hear,' Fang told her, 'he went around all the setts killing the badgers. Foxes too, when he found them.'

'The last time we went on a journey,' said Hop-along, 'we met two badgers and they told us a similar story. They had come from the Land of the Cow. Their setts had been destroyed and many of their kind wiped out.'

'They said some of their kind had got a sickness from the cows,' Old Sage Brush recalled, 'but it seemed to me that perhaps man thought his cows had got the sickness from the badgers.'

'Well, whatever way it is,' continued Fang, 'I just wanted to warn you – keep away from this farm. There's a dead cow in one of the fields, and dead badgers in the ditches.'

'Yes, we saw the cow,' said Little Running Fox, 'and we were wondering what had happened to it. Do you think it was the sickness that killed it?'

Fang shook his head. 'I don't know. I saw man dragging it out of a stream. Maybe it just drowned.'

'Well, he can hardly blame the badgers for that,' said Scat, embarrassed now at having suggested to his friends that the cow might have been killed by a giant ginger cat.

Twinkle, who felt equally silly for having thought it could have been the work of a wolf, added, 'And he can't blame foxes.'

'Maybe not,' Fang told them, 'but he may well have lost other cows to the sickness, or lambs to a fox. So you would be well advised to stay away.'

There was silence as the young foxes thought of the danger they had been in.

'Anyway,' Fang went on, 'there's a billy goat over there, and if he butts you with those horns of his you'll feel as if you've been kicked by a horse.'

Young Black Tip, who had still not said a word about what had happened to him at the farm, glanced at his friends out of the corner of his eye. They were, he could see, trying to suppress smiles, but he kept a straight face and said nothing.

'Which reminds me,' added Fang. 'There was a horse in the field the last time you stopped. I saw it snuffling around your earth during the night. You must have wondered what it was.'

'We were sound asleep,' said Hop-along. 'We didn't hear a thing.'

The young foxes gave one another a knowing look. This time they were all smiling, but again they hid their foolishness by remaining silent.

'Tell me, Fang,' said Scat, more to get away from the subject than anything else, 'did you go to the Land of the Giant Ginger Cats too?'

Fang nodded, and Old Sage Brush said, 'Of course he did. And what's more, if it hadn't been for Fang we wouldn't have got back. The fun dogs were waiting for us, and he drew them off.'

Now it was Fang's turn to be embarrassed, so he changed the subject by saying, 'What do you think the badgers mean when they talk about going to the Valley of the Dragon?'

'Who knows,' said the old fox. 'But first things first. I think we've had too much talk about giants and dragons. The truth is, the only giants we'll find around here are horses and cows, and they are harmless as far as we are concerned. I had hoped that we would have met some badgers by now who would have told us how far we are from the Fragrant Wood. But it appears man has decided that badgers and cows cannot live together here either. So we must press on.'

'Do you mind if I come?' asked Fang.

Old Sage Brush smiled. 'I was hoping you would.'

The call of the cuckoo continued to drift across the countryside, but whether it was one bird or several the foxes had no way of knowing. While Ratwiddle had come in to join them, he still stayed apart, and Old Sage Brush asked Fang to keep an eye on him in case he might bring trouble upon them or himself. Happy to help, yet not wishing to end up with fleas, Fang stayed as near his eccentric friend as he dared. He also took the opportunity to try and talk to him.

As a fox who had never shied away from a fight, Fang was particularly interested in what Ratwiddle had said about foxes running from the wolf. Hares were fast but he was confident he could run down the best of them. Flames, he recalled, always ran to the sky and were best avoided. But foxes running from the wolf? That really puzzled him. Foxlore, he knew, did speak of wolves, but that was a long time ago. Man, they were told, had hunted the wolf, but the wolf hadn't run fast enough and now it was no more. What, then, had prompted Ratwiddle to speak of the wolf? Time and again Fang tried to communicate with him, but his mind was too far away and there was no way Fang could reach it.

Fang himself had no problem in opening up his own mind, and at night, when they were resting, regaled the young foxes with stories of his adventures in far-flung fields. Somehow Scat suspected that unlike himself, Fang had enjoyed many adventures with beautiful young vixens, and he decided that some time, when they were alone together, he would ask Fang to tell him more about them.

For his part, Young Black Tip was still feeling stiff and sore, and he was grateful when Ratwiddle went off on his own again and Fang began to help him with the hunting. If Fang had seen him being butted by the billy-goat, he never mentioned it and for that the young fox was even more grateful. Soon his feelings, which had been as badly bruised as his hindquarters, began to heal and, like the other young foxes, he was glad Fang had decided to come along with them.

SIX

The Year of the Cock

As Little Running Fox continued to pick out the markers that would lead them to the badgers, they came to the bank of a wide, fast-flowing river. A narrow wooden footbridge took them over it and they found themselves looking across a meadow covered with buttercups.

Horses with fine legs and fancy white fetlocks, which suggested speed rather than strength, grazed quietly in the meadow. Moving slowly among the flowers, the horses flicked their tails now and then to dislodge flies and other insects that had chosen to feed upon them. In the buttercups themselves, bumblebees foraged for pollen, oblivious to the larks that sang above them or the grey heron that stood motionless at the edge of the river. The round, yellow-ringed eye of the heron was watching for fish, but the movement of the foxes as they made their way quietly through the rushes and dock leaves did not escape its attention.

Beyond the meadow was a wood of stately oak, sycamore and beech. In the tops of the trees rooks nested in noisy ever-changing colonies, and down below, the foxes found, badgers were asleep in the depths of their setts.

The huge spreading trees were interspersed with exotic species of tall tapering evergreens and shaded walks. Twinkle sniffed the sweet scent of pine and said, 'I wonder if this is it – the Fragrant Wood?'

A badger, whom the older foxes had roused from his sleep, chuckled and told her, 'Fragrant it may be, but safe it is not. Better come below ground. We can talk there.'

Young Black Tip and Scat, however, were exploring their new surroundings, looking up at the trees with wonder and sniffing the ground with great interest. Having wandered away from the others, they had come upon a very strong scent, stronger indeed than anything they had ever experienced before. It was, they knew, the scent of a bird, and when they followed it, they found that it led to the most magnificent bird they had ever seen.

Without warning the strange bird swooped from the trees. Gliding on outspread wings, it had a long floating tail and claws that hung below, ready, it seemed, to clutch at its prey. Mesmerised, the young foxes could only stand and watch. Never had they seen the like of it before, but it matched exactly the image they had of the huge birds of prey their parents had told them about. Fortunately, this one wasn't swooping on them or on any prey. Its claws were only spread in readiness for landing, and when it came to a halt it did a most amazing thing. Wiggling its rear in a sort of shivering movement, its long trailing tail shot up in the air, then fanned out like a rainbow in a dazzling display of colour.

Brilliant blue – or was it purple? This magical bird seemed to have all the elusive hues that sparkled in the head of the drake, the neck of the pheasant, the breast of the starling, the back of the kingfisher and the tail of the magpie. And in its great spreading tail were all the eyes they had ever seen on the wings of butterflies. As they marvelled at its beauty and size, for it was truly a giant among birds, it raised its tufted head and uttered a call that was unusually harsh and not at all in keeping with its colour.

Young Black Tip and Scat took a step back and, almost too late, realised that the harsh call of the rainbow bird was a warning, for there, racing through the trees towards them, were two of the biggest hounds they had ever seen. Taller than calves, faster than the howling dogs, they were bearing down on the foxes with incredible speed.

Springing into action, the two young foxes turned and using muscles they never even knew they had, sprinted for the safety of the badger sett. With every bound they took, they could hear the long legs of the giant dogs eating up the space behind them. The sett they could see, was still some little distance away. The hounds were almost on them, so tall they seemed to be panting and slavering above them. Now they could feel the breath from the jaws as they opened up to grab them, and for one terrifying moment it seemed they wouldn't make it. Then, to their indescribable relief, the mouth of the badger sett loomed up before them and they plunged inside.

The rainbow birds, the badgers assured their visitors, were noisy and bad-tempered, even fearless, but posed no danger. They would wander through the trees, or strut across the lawns, and they seemed to have no other purpose in life than to add colour to the estate. Occasionally, as if to show off, they would fan out their tails in all their glory, making the daffodils or the rhododendrons, or whatever other flowers were in bloom, seem dull by comparison. They seemed to be able to come and go as they pleased, and man didn't seem to mind, even when they perched on the highest pinnacle of his home and crowed about it.

In fact, the badgers' impressions of what the young foxes called 'the rainbow bird' weren't far wrong. In times long past, these birds had been given as cherished gifts to kings and emperors. Then man had brought them from far distant lands to grace the lawns of the stately homes of Europe. Known to him as peacocks, they gave a splash of colour to a domain whose native birds were anything but colourful.

The hounds, on the other hand, had been a feature of the big houses for even longer. Natives of the country from time immemorial, they too had been given as gifts to kings and princes. Having hunted for man until they had nothing more of their size to hunt, they were known to him by the same name as they were known to the badger. 'Unlike the fox,' one of the badgers explained, 'we stay in one place. We've had setts here for longer than anyone can remember and from the knowledge that has been handed down from one generation to another, we know that the giant hounds once hunted the wolf.'

'You mean, they're wolfhounds?' asked Young lack Tip.

The badgers nodded their striped heads, and one of them confirmed, 'That's what we call them.'

'So now they're hunting us,' said Little Running Fox.

'And if they've hunted the wolf out of existence,' Hop-along remarked, 'what hope have we got?'

'At least Ratwiddle tried to warn us,' said Twinkle.

'Anyway,' Fang told them, 'we outran the fun dogs remember?'

The old fox corrected him. '*You* did.'

'And we outran the howling dogs,' said Scat.

Young Black Tip looked at him. 'We almost didn't. It was a close-run thing.'

Twinkle got up and went over to lie down beside her grandfather.

'I must say, I got a terrible fright,' admitted Scat. 'I mean, Old Sage Brush said there was no such thing as giants any more. At least, not outside man's place.'

Old Sage Brush grunted. 'So I did.' He sighed. 'So I did. But then, I suppose, even a squirrel can fall from a tree.

Scat leaned over to his mother and whispered, 'What does he mean, even a squirrel can fall from a tree?'

'I think,' She-la told him, 'he means, anyone can make a mistake.'

Fang turned to the badgers. 'Tell me,' he said, 'if the wolfhounds are so dangerous, how come you have survived here for so long?'

That was something the other foxes hadn't thought of and, lifting their heads, they waited expectantly to hear what the badgers had to say.

'It's very simple,' replied one of the badgers. 'Most of us, especially our young, only go out at night when the wolfhounds are locked in.'

'But if the wolfhounds only come out during the day,' asked Young Black Tip, 'how do you know so much about them?'

'As you know,' the badger told him, 'our eyesight is not good, but even from within our sett we cannot fail to see them. Nor can we fail to notice the colours of the big bird as it struts around outside.'

'How could they live here for so long and not know about them?' the old fox observed. 'Anyway, we've come upon a dangerous path. Let's hope that when darkness comes, we'll be able to leave by a safer one.'

Being aware of the purpose of their journey, the badgers made the foxes welcome, and it was only as they talked that it emerged that the badger who had called to see Old Sage Brush at the oak tree had not come from the Fragrant Wood. As the badgers themselves had pointed out, they were not accustomed to travelling far, and so the request from those who lived in the Fragrant Wood had come not by one messenger covering a long distance, but by word of mouth passed on from one sett to another.

As the other foxes talked to the badgers and tried to find out what the problem was at the Fragrant Wood, Young Black Tip and Scat withdrew to a side chamber.

'What do you think?' whispered Scat.

I don't know,' his friend replied. 'I suppose if we get across the river tonight and put enough space between us and the wolfhounds, we should be all right.'

'But can we get far enough from them in one night?' wondered Scat. 'I mean, Hop-along can't go very fast, and Old Sage Brush is just as slow . . . Not to mention Ratwiddle. I don't know what we're going to do about him. Dear knows where he is.'

Young Black Tip took a deep breath. 'We'll just have to try. I've four cubs waiting for me at home – not to mention a lovely vixen.'

'What's that you say about a lovely vixen?' They looked up to see that Fang had come to join them. It was the opportunity Scat had been waiting for and, forgetting about the wolfhounds for a moment, he got Fang to tell them about some of the vixens he had met on his travels.

In another chamber nearby, Little Running Fox and Twinkle were also discussing their dilemma. More than once, they knew, Old Sage Brush and Hop-along had escaped from the dogs that hunted for fun, but even a strong fox like Fang would be no match for the giant hounds that had chased the wolf.

After a while, the badgers went to sleep again, and never a one to waste an opportunity, Old Sage Brush did the same. For the other foxes, time seemed to pass very slowly, and then, almost as if he had heard it in his sleep, the old fox woke to a familiar sound. It was the call of an owl somewhere out in the woods. At the same time, the badgers were stirring. It was, he knew, time to be on their way.

Moving quietly through the darkened woods, the foxes made their way back down through the Meadow of Buttercups. Like the wolfhounds, the horses had been taken in for the night, and a short time later Little Running Fox led the way over the footbridge. Fang was the last to go over, and with the river between them and the big house, they all felt much safer.

Pausing to look back, they saw the dark outline of a rainbow bird perched on the topmost turret of the big house. At the same time they heard a deep-throated howl rising above the trees. It wasn't the howl of dogs that hunted with red-coated riders, or the howl of dogs that hunted for fun, but a howl so deep it could only have come from a giant hound. Thinking that perhaps it was howling at the wide eye of gloomglow, Fang looked up, only to see that a canopy of cloud covered the night sky, and he knew the hound was howling at them. Almost immediately another hound joined in, and the two howled together in a chilling cry that sent a shiver of fear through the foxes. Hoping that the hounds had in fact been locked in for the night, they hurried away.

By the time the first rays of dawn had begun to brighten the horizon, the foxes were safely settled in an earth deep in a patch of gorse. They were tired, and soon they were all asleep with the exception of Fang. Tired, but uneasy, he slipped out and made his way to a hill from which he could look back at the Land of the Wolfhound. The Meadow of Buttercups, he could see, was shrouded in an early morning mist. Slowly the sun began to burn the mist from the river and as it cleared away he saw, to his dismay, the two giant hounds galloping across the footbridge towards him.

SEVEN

The Year of the Wolf

The soft call of the cuckoo could once again be heard, spreading softly and as always secretly, across the countryside. While others slept, Old Sage Brush lay at the mouth of the earth, enjoying the early morning sun. 'I can see the summer coming,' he told Twinkle. 'I imagine it's very nice.'

His grand-daughter, who was lying beside him, looked out across the rolling fields. 'It's lovely,' she confirmed. 'The sky is blue, only a few white clouds. The grass is long and shiny and some of the fields are in stripes where man has rolled them. The gorse is still in bloom, dandelions are popping up everywhere, and there are so many daisies now you couldn't walk without stepping on one.'

'Is the hawthorn still in bloom?' asked the old fox.

'The hedges are still white and pink with blossoms,' Twinkle informed him. 'But the flowers are coming on the elderberry now and it won't be long before they take over.'

As Twinkle surveyed the countryside, she saw for the first time that lacy fronds of cow parsley were spreading along the hedgerows.

'And what is that I feel touching my nose?' asked the old fox.

Seeing that it was a long arching briar, Twinkle told him, 'It's the stem of the summer rose.'

Remembering that the flowers of the briar were pale pink, the old fox asked, 'Are the roses on it yet?'

'Not yet,' Twinkle replied. 'It's the new leaves that are tickling your nose.'

'And the buttercups?' continued Old Sage Brush 'Are there many of them?'

Suspecting that the old fox was thinking of the Meadow of Buttercups, Twinkle just said, 'Some.' But if she was hoping to divert his mind from their recent experience in the Land of the Wolfhound, she was wasting her time.

Suddenly, Fang came racing up to the earth. 'It's the wolfhounds,' he panted.

'Are they coming after us?' asked the old fox.

'I'm not sure.' Fang lay down and waited to get his breath back. 'But they've crossed the river.'

Old Sage Brush got up and went into the earth. Twinkle looked at Fang, and seeing nothing in his eyes that offered any form of reassurance, also hurried inside. Soon a babble of voices filled the earth as news of what Fang had seen spread, and sensing their consternation, the old fox called them to order.

'Fang,' he said, 'is there any way we can outrun the wolfhounds?'

Fang shook his head. 'It's not possible.'

'Could you do it on your own?' asked the old fox.

'Not even on my own,' replied Fang.

Young Black Tip and Scat, who had felt the breath of the hounds on the back of their necks, confirmed that the long legs of the giant dogs could eat up the ground with amazing speed.

'Maybe,' said She-la, more to comfort her mate than anything else, 'maybe they're not coming after us.'

'But what if they come upon us?' argued Hop-along. 'What do we do then? If Fang couldn't outrun them, what hope would I have?'

'Or I?' said the old fox.

'Then we must do what you have taught us to do,' said Little Running Fox. 'We must think.'

Old Sage Brush smiled. 'Good thinking, little one. Now, what we have to figure out is this. What can we do that the wolfhound cannot do? Where can we go that the wolfhound cannot go? Most of all, what have we got that the wolfhound has not got?'

'The giant hound is tall,' said Scat. 'But we are nimble.'

The old fox nodded.

'It's fast,' said Young Black Tip. 'But it cannot follow us into an earth.'

'It may have hunted the wolf,' said Fang, 'but from what I saw of it this morning, it doesn't hunt with its nose. Otherwise it would have found us by now.'

'So it's like the gazehound that chases the hare,' said Hop-along. 'It hunts by sight.'

'If that is so,' suggested She-la, 'then we should travel by night.'

'If we travel by night,' Little Running Fox pointed out 'we will not find the markers that will lead us to the Fragrant Wood.'

'Then we must do the next best thing,' Old Sage Brush told them. 'We must use all the cover that is available to us and hope the wolfhounds will not see us.

Unknown to the foxes, they had correctly identified some of the characteristics of the tallest dog in the world. Originally bred as hunters of wolves and deer, the hounds that were causing them concern were members of a family known to man and fox as gazehounds. Like the one man now called, the greyhound, the wolfhound hunted by sight. And had the foxes known and understood what man had once written about it, they would have been more concerned:

The flower of all his race,
So true, so brave, a lamb at home
A lion in the chase.

Fortunately, the foxes were unaware of the finer characteristics of man and the poetic sentiments he sometimes expressed. All they knew was that the dog with which man had once hunted the wolf was out there somewhere and they could not run the risk of being caught in the open. As they continued their journey, therefore, they kept to the ditches and streams – especially where they were covered by hedgerows – crossed fields only where there were patches of gorse and scrub, and ventured into open meadows only where the red of their fur blended with the russet of the dock.

By scouting the land ahead of them, Little Running Fox was able to steer them on a safe path, and by scouting the land behind, Fang and Scat were able to keep an eye on the two wolfhounds. The hounds were there all right, some distance back, and often, it would seem, they were just amusing themselves. Sometimes, Fang would tell the others, he had seen the two big hounds playing like fox cubs, rolling on the ground, nipping each other and engaging in short mock chases. On other occasions, Scat would report that he had seen the two hounds galloping down a hedgerow at an incredible speed. It was, he said, as if they were chasing after a rabbit they had seen, although they always seemed to give up when they skidded to the spot where the rabbit had been.

So long as the foxes were able to keep out of sight, they knew they were safe, but soon their travels brought them to a large expanse of farmland from which all gorse and scrub had long since been cleared.

'Can we not go around it?' asked Old Sage Brush when Little Running Fox came back to report her predicament.

'We could all right,' she replied. 'But we might never find the next marker.'

'What sort of farmland is it?' asked Fang.

'Bare fields with cattle in them,' the little fox replied. 'No cover at all.'

'Any crops?' asked Hop-along, who, because of his handicap, always sought out any cover he could find.

'Beyond the grazing fields,' replied Little Running Fox. 'There are some barley fields.'

'And beyond them?' asked the old fox.

'A mountain.'

The others waited expectantly as Old Sage Brush considered what she had told them. 'What height is the barley?' he asked. 'I mean, is it as high as a fox?'

Little Running Fox stood up so that she could measure herself against Fang, who was the tallest, and said, 'I only saw it from a distance, mind you, but I think it's a bit taller than we are.'

'Well, Hop-along,' said the old fox, 'what do you think?'

Hop-along took a deep breath. 'I suppose if Scat and Fang tell us when it's safe to go, we might make it.'

'But how do we know what will be over there when we do go?' asked She-la, forever concerned, not for her own safety, but for the safety of her three-legged mate.

'Well, one thing's for sure,' said Old Sage Brush. 'We can't go back.'

There was no arguing with that, so as soon as Fang and Scat reported that the two giant hounds were far enough back and amusing themselves wherever their curiosity took them, Little Running Fox led the others at a brisk trot across the grazing fields. However, the foxes had forgotten that cows too are curious creatures. Seeing so many foxes crossing the fields, the cows began to run after them, some mooing loudly in the process.

Whatever about their sense of smell, there was nothing wrong with the wolfhounds' hearing. Abandoning the rabbits, or whatever else had taken their fancy, they raced towards the sound of the cows. By this time the cows had come to a halt, and seeing the foxes fleeing across the fields, the two hounds immediately gave chase. Looking back, Fang and Scat saw the hounds coming up the fields after them at a frightening speed, their ears flapping, their long tails curled above them.

Casting a quick glance ahead, Fang knew immediately that Old Sage Brush and Hop-along weren't going to make it. The younger foxes knew it too. Almost without thinking, Fang barked at Young Black Tip, 'You stay with them, we'll try and draw them off!'

Turning to Scat, Fang told him, 'You run for that hedge, I'll take the other one.'

The two immediately peeled off, and seeing them go in different directions, the wolfhounds also split up and galloped after them in hot pursuit.

Soon Fang knew exactly how Young Black Tip and Scat had felt the day they had raced for the badger sett. He could hear one of the giant hounds thudding after him as its massive pads pounded the mud, its long legs covering the ground with strides he could not match. He could hear it panting loudly now, salivating at the thought of a kill. With one last mighty effort, he threw himself in under the hedge. Too big to follow, the hound skidded to a stop. For a moment it ran up and down searching for him, then turned to see how its companion had done.

Fang was relieved to see that Scat too had escaped by a hair's breadth, and for the first time he was able to observe the hounds at close quarters. The one that had chased Scat was fawn-coloured, his own pursuer dark grey, and both had long beards above and below their mouths. They were panting heavily and their tongues, which were lolling out over their long pointed teeth, were dribbling so profusely that their beards were matted and wet.

Suddenly the giant hounds turned away from the foxes they had lost, and bounded up the field in pursuit of Old Sage Brush, Hop-along and the others. Emerging from the hedge, Fang joined up with Scat. To their great relief, they saw that the rest of the group had already disappeared into a field of barley. Little Running Fox, they were glad to see, had guessed correctly: the barley was high enough to cover them. But the giant hounds were bounding through the young stalks looking for them.

Now began a game of hide-and-seek which would have gone down in the folklore of man had he been privileged to see it. On entering the barley field, Little Running Fox discovered that there were several rows of narrow tracks running up it. These, she reckoned, had been left by the wheels of man's machines when he had sown his seeds. Realising that any movement of the barley would bring the giant hounds down upon them, she led her little group up one of these tracks, at the same time barking to some of the others to try and draw the hounds away.

Without hesitation, She-la and Young Black Tip dashed off through the barley, heading blindly for the nearest hedge. The two hounds, who were some way down the field, immediately stopped and cocked their ears. They had heard the rustle of the stalks and now, seeing the movement of the seed-heads, they raced through the barley towards them. So tall were the hounds that the young barley didn't even reach their bellies, but it did slow them down – not very much, it must be said, but long enough for the two foxes to reach the hedge.

Thwarted once again, the giant hounds milled around the hedgerow. As they did so, they heard the rustle of running foxes from the far side of the field, and immediately bounded away towards them. This time, Fang and Scat slipped under a patch of briars with relative ease. Again the hounds lingered, but only for a moment. Then they heard foxes on the other side of the field again, but when they got there, She-la and Young Black Tip had taken cover once more.

So it went on until, at last, the giant hounds could run no more. With their tongues lolling out and their long hairy bellies heaving with exhaustion, they lay down in the barley which, by now, was trampled almost flat. Weary from the chase, they closed their large brown eyes and, perhaps, dreamed of the time their ancestors had chased a quarry that was big enough to see. For them the chase was over, at least for one day.

EIGHT

The Year of the Hare

Since leaving the Land of Sinna, Old Sage Brush and his friends had taken a path that was not of their own choosing. It had entailed crossing several roads, or as the foxes called them, man's pathways, and that was something they preferred to avoid. Man's machines, they knew, were much faster and less predictable than other creatures. They came hurtling out of nowhere and caused many casualties, especially when young foxes were striking out on their own.

Dangerous as it might be for foxes, hedgehogs and badgers found it even more difficult to avoid these machines. They suffered a lot of casualties, or so it seemed to Little Running Fox. Scouting ahead, she had come to another of man's pathways and was looking at the bodies of two young badgers lying at the edge of it. Flies were buzzing around them and, pausing for a moment to look at them, the little fox was saddened to think that they had been struck down almost before they had found their own path in life.

Concerned lest any of her group might end up the same way, Little Running Fox searched along the side of the road until she came to a place where it went in under a large gaping hole in the shape of an arching briar. On each side of the hole the fields rose steeply, and climbing to the top, she found that another pathway crossed over the one below. Whatever it had been used for in the past, the signs told her that the upper pathway was no longer used by man's machines, only by his cattle. What a pity, she thought, that the badgers and hedgehogs had chosen such a dangerous place to cross when here, only a short distance away, was a crossing they could have used with comparative safety. Fetching her friends, she led them over it and soon they were making their way up into the foothills of the mountain. A short time later a farmer walked across the ancient stone bridge, as he did every evening, but the only tracks he saw were those of his cattle.

There was little or no cover in the hills, and fearing that the wolfhounds might spot them again, the foxes sought out a hollow where they could rest without the risk of being seen. It was coming on to dusk now, and Old Sage Brush was dozing when She-la came over to talk to him.

'I am worried about Hop-along,' She-la confided in him

The old fox nodded. 'I know, he must be tired. But we're almost there.'

'He's tired all right,' She-la told him. 'But that's not what he's worried about.'

Even though he couldn't see her, the old fox turned his head towards her. 'What is it then?' he asked.

'It's what Ratwiddle said, about the hares.'

Sage Brush grunted. 'Ratwiddle? Sure he hasn't been seen for a long time. Anyway, all he said was that he could see hares running with the flowers.'

'I know,' said She-la. 'But anything Ratwiddle sees always spells danger for us.'

'I don't see how there can be any danger in the flowers.' said the old fox.

'It's not the flowers he's worried about,' continued She-la.

'It's the mountain hares. Remember the experience he had with them once before?'

Old Sage Brush smiled. 'How could I forget? But what is he worried about? He outwitted the best of them, didn't he? It worked like a dream!'

She-la was silent, and sensing that she needed some form of reassurance, the old fox told her, 'All right so. If you're that worried, tell Fang to check around and see if there are any hares about.' Hearing She-la getting up to go, he added, 'And tell him to keep an eye out for Ratwiddle. I just hope the hounds haven't got him.'

Word of what Fang was doing soon came to the ears of the younger foxes, and they were particularly intrigued. Many times they had heard the story of how, before they were born, their parents had been stopped in the hills by a great gathering of hares. With one fox blind and another having only three legs, it must have been a nightmare. Yet, with only cunning to help him, Hop-along had reached for the very eye of gloomglow and out-jumped the leader of the hares, Lepus the

Great. It was a story that had gone down in foxlore, to be told and retold to each new generation of foxes.

Fang, it was said, had also been there, but it was the weakest whom Old Sage Brush had chosen to deal with the hares. Now he had chosen the strongest, but when Fang returned to the hollow, it was to report that he had seen no hares at all.

Old Sage Brush was glad, but the truth was he had a more serious problem on his mind. How, he wondered, were they going to get across the bare hills and over the mountain without being seen by the giant hounds? Until they could come up with an answer, they would have to stay put. They would also have to eat, and if there were no hares to be found they would have to look for rabbits.

Since Fang had been out most of the night, Young Black Tip was sent out to hunt. Acting on the old fox's instructions, he kept to streams and gullies and whenever possible to the sides of hills where he wouldn't be seen by the wolfhounds. He caught two rabbits, which he hid for collection later, and was searching for a third when he put up a hare. The hare had been lying in its form, a nest that was covered over by long bending grass, and it waited until the last minute before breaking cover.

Young Black Tip immediately gave chase, but soon realised that the hare was strong and fast. Twisting and turning, it eluded his grasp on numerous occasions. Eventually it drew away from him, and disappeared over a small rise. When Young Black Tip reached the spot, the hare was nowhere to be seen. He then realised he was back where he had started, and went over to the form to investigate. To his surprise, the hare bolted from the form once more, and the chase started all over again. Unlike Young Black Tip, however, the hare showed no sign of tiredness and he lost it a second time.

If the other young foxes had been intrigued by Hop-along's story, they were now intrigued by the one told by Young Black Tip. Little Running Fox went out to try her luck, and when she came back with a similar story, Scat went out, then Twinkle. They had no success either, and now it was the turn of the older foxes to be intrigued.

Once again, Fang was asked to investigate and, fast as he was, he also found the mountain hares to be faster. He reckoned he could have caught the one he put up, but for the fact that it always escaped from him long enough to get a short rest, with the result that it seemed to remain fresh while he got more and more tired. Finally he lay down to rest himself and consider the situation.

Having been up most of the night, Fang dozed off, and when he awoke he saw to his surprise that Ratwiddle had arrived. But what really surprised him was that while Ratwiddle was sitting on the side of a hill scratching himself, he was being watched by a hare. The hare was sitting on its haunches nearby, and seemed to have no fear of him. Puzzled, Fang eased himself up and walked slowly over to them.

Stopping as close to Ratwiddle as he could without getting fleas, and as near to the hare as he dared without frightening it off, Fang lay down. When he had settled, the hare looked at him with one of its big brown eyes, and said, 'If you kill me you will die.'

'How do you mean, I will die?' asked Fang.

'Because,' said the hare, twitching its nose, 'you cannot cross the mountain without my help.'

Fang snorted. 'I don't need the help of a hare to cross a mountain. I can find my own way.'

'Only by day can you find your way across,' the hare continued, 'and then the wolfhounds will see you.'

Fang shrugged. 'We'll go by night.'

'You'll never find your way by night,' the hare told him. 'It is too dangerous.'

'My friend here,' said Fang, nodding to Ratwiddle, 'has seen the hares running with the flowers. He's a bit strange.'

'I see nothing strange about him,' replied the hare. 'And he's right, we do run with the flowers.'

Fang took a deep breath. The hare was talking in riddles, just like Ratwiddle. He had often seen hares dancing together at mating time, and considered them to be a bit mad. Maybe, he thought, this hare was strange in the same way that Ratwiddle was. At the same time, he reckoned it might be better to keep his thoughts to himself, so he just said, 'How can you run with the flowers?'

The hare grinned. 'Because when we run the flowers run with us.' Seeing that Fang was perplexed, the hare explained, 'You see, we are the flowers. We take our names from them. I thought everyone knew that'.

Fang shook his head. 'I didn't.

'Well, we do. My name is Harebell'.

'You run very fast,' Fang remarked.

'We have to,' said Harebell. 'You see, the wolfhound chases us too'.

'But how can you run so fast?' asked Fang. 'I mean, without getting tired?'

Harebell smiled. 'That is the way we outrun the wolfhound. It's a secret that has been handed down from one generation of hares to another. Surely you wouldn't expect us to share it with the fox?'

Fang smiled too. 'I suppose not. But what are you proposing?'

'It's very simple,' Harebell told him. 'You know you cannot catch us, so you cannot kill us. But in trying to do so, you run the risk of drawing the giant hounds upon us – and upon yourselves.'

Fang nodded, and the hare continued, 'So what we are proposing is this. You stop chasing us and we will take you safely across the mountain. There we'll arrange for one of the badgers to meet you and take you to the Fragrant Wood.'

'You know of the Fragrant Wood then?' asked Fang.

'Of course,' said Harebell 'And we know why you are going there. Ratwiddle told us.'

Fang sighed. How, he wondered, could Ratwiddle have understood what they were doing, and how could he have communicated with the hares when he couldn't communicate with other foxes? Unless, he thought again, the hares were as mad as Ratwiddle was.

And yet, what Harebell was saying made a lot of sense. Fang got up to go. 'All right,' he said, 'I'll discuss it with my friends and let you know.'

Back in the hollow, Old Sage Brush and the others listened, entranced, as Fang related what the hare had told him.

'Harebell, you say?' The old fox lifted his head as if he was seeing something in his mind's eye. 'If my memory serves me right, that's a lovely blue flower.'

She-la nodded. 'Bigger than a bluebell, but with a more slender stem.'

'And where's Ratwiddle now?' asked the old fox.

Fang was frustrated. 'I don't know. Out there somewhere. But don't worry. He can look after himself, although how he does it, I'll never know.'

'From what you say,' said Old Sage Brush, 'it seems to me he is more at home with the hares than he is with us.'

Having been asked for their opinion, the young foxes agreed with Fang: what Harebell had said made a lot of sense.

'And you, Hop-along?' asked the old fox.

Hop-along got up and hobbled over beside him. 'If we can't outrun the wolfhound, and we can't overtake the hare, what hope have we of crossing the mountain on our own?'

'And don't forget,' said She-la, 'we also have to come back.'

Old Sage Brush turned to Fang. 'That settles it then. Tell Harebell we agree.'

When the moon had crept into the sky above the mountain, and bathed the land in the half-light which the foxes know as gloomglow, a strange meeting took place in the hollow. Traditional enemies, the foxes and hares sat around in a circle and talked as friends. Even Ratwiddle was there but if he could talk to the hares, he didn't do so.

'There is only one way you can get across the mountain without being seen,' Harebell told the foxes. 'And that's when it's raining. But you must be in position and ready to go in case the rain doesn't last long.'

'How will we know when it's going to rain?' asked Little Running Fox.

Harebell smiled. 'I told you. We are named after the flowers. With me here are Daisy, Primrose, Bindweed, and Dandelion.'

'And how will that help?' asked Young Black Tip.

'Some of the flowers don't like the rain,' Harebell explained. 'So they close up when it is on the way.'

'But the primroses have gone,' said Twinkle. 'And the bindweed has not yet come into flower.'

Harebell smiled again. 'True, but the daisy and the dandelion are always with us, and never more so than now.'

If, in the days that followed, man had seen a fox in the foothills hunting for rabbits, he would have noticed that it seemed to take an inordinate interest in flowers. He might even have examined the flowers himself to see what was of such great interest to the fox.

However, it would never have occurred to him that the fox was merely looking to see if the flowers were open or closed.

In fact, it seemed to the foxes that some of the flowers were always closed, some were half-closed, and some closed as the daylight faded. But then they weren't used to looking at flowers. The hares were, and when Dandelion told the foxes it was time to go, they didn't hesitate.

A mist had closed in around the mountain, and soon it began to rain. With a sureness of foot that only a mountain goat could match, Harebell and her friends led the foxes along a series of paths and ledges known only to themselves. These secret paths, it seemed to the foxes, also took them more around the mountain than over it. By the time they arrived on the far side, the weather had cleared, and they scanned the foothills for the badger who was to meet them. Beyond the foothills lay a valley that stretched away as far as the eye could see. Part of it was bog, part of it farmland. One patch, however, was neither. There, it seemed, man had scooped up all the hedges and stones of the countryside and dumped them in one place.

'What's that?' asked Little Running Fox.

'That,' Harebell told them, 'is all that remains of the Fragrant Wood.'

PART TWO

'The sweetest bird on the branches singing,
The cuckoo on top of the green hill;
And death shall never find us
In the bosom of the fragrant wood.'

From an old Gaelic poem

NINE

The Year of the Serpent

From what the young badger told him, Old Sage Brush reckoned that the trees had been very old – as old, probably, as the ancient oak under which he lived in the Land of Sinna. When Harebell had said goodbye on the lower slopes of the mountain, the badger brought them down to see all that was left of what he, and the hares, lovingly called the Fragrant Wood. But what had once been a wild wood was now a scene of utter devastation. Using his great machines, the badger told them, man had gouged it out of the ground. One night it was there. The next it was gone, and so were the setts, setts that were as old as the trees themselves.

As the other foxes looked out across the wasteland that had once been a wood, they told the old fox everything they saw. And they spoke in hushed voices, for they were appalled at what man had done. For a short time they had enjoyed the stately woods beside the Meadow of Buttercups, and now as they looked at the sawn-up remains of the badgers' home, they tried to imagine how it had been.

This had been an even more ancient wood, but now almost all the trees were gone – tall spreading oaks that had sheltered many creatures besides the badgers, hardy ash and silver birch which, like the oaks, had hosted generations of rooks, magpies and pigeons, and, on the fringes, alders and hazels under which squirrels and jays had hidden nuts and acorns. All gone. Only the stumps remained, and even they had been torn up by the roots and piled in heaps. Elsewhere, a tangle of twigs and branches, which weren't worth removing, littered the forest floor. The only things left standing were the weaklings of the forest, a few long stringy trees that had failed to flourish in the shade. Stripped of their support, they now stood in an ungainly fashion, swaying to and fro in the summer breeze.

'Where do we go from here?' asked Little Running Fox.

'Follow me,' said the young badger, and they hurried after him.

The badger led them across the fields and into the bog they had seen from the foothills. It was, as they had seen, a big area of bog, and it had been worked extensively by man and his machines. However, one small part of it remained intact. This was a low hill on which stood the ruins of a building put there by man in the dim distant past.

'That's where they live now,' said the young badger. 'Where man used to live.'

Young Black Tip was still looking at it. 'I can't see them – I mean, your friends.'

'Don't worry,' the young badger told them. 'They're still there. You see, they can't leave.'

Old Sage Brush, who couldn't see, asked Twinkle, 'What does he mean, they can't leave?'

'It's surrounded by water,' she told him.

'When their homes were destroyed,' the young badger explained, 'they ran to the hill. There they dug new setts and hid from man. Then one day they found they couldn't leave.'

The young badger lay down and the foxes did likewise. 'You see, there had been no rain for a long time and everything was very dry. Then the rains came, and they woke up to find they were surrounded by water.'

'How did you get out then?' asked Fang.

'I was already out,' said the young badger. 'I couldn't get back in. Then one night, another young badger succeeded in swimming over to us – there are other badgers on this side, you understand. He asked us to send a message from their leader to the foxes in the Land of Sinna. The young badger was half drowned, and he died soon afterwards, but at least he got the message out, and we passed it on from one sett to another.' He paused, before adding, 'Thanks for coming.'

'What's the point?' asked Scat. 'If we can't get over to them?'

Fang stood up and looked across at the island. 'Maybe we could swim over.'

'Even if we could get over there,' said She-la, 'they can't get over here, so we'd just be wasting our time.'

Old Sage Brush had heard enough. 'All right, badger,' he said, 'we'll think about it.'

The young badger thanked them again and left. His work was done. It was up to the foxes.

The bog didn't go right up to the water's edge, they discovered. There was a grassy slope in between on which grew a tangle of briars and blackthorn. These were interlaced at the bottom with long withered grass and weeds, and provided ideal cover. The undergrowth also contained a strong tangle of scents, indicating the presence of rabbits, waterhens, and snipe in the vicinity, and with the approach of dusk, Old Sage Brush sent the young foxes out to hunt. At the same time, he asked Fang and She-la to go around the island and see if there was any way they might be able to get across the water.

Fang went one way, She-la the other, and when they returned they confirmed what the young badger had told them. There was no way across.

'Any sign of the badgers?' asked Hop-along.

She-la nodded. 'Once, when I looked across the water, I got a glimpse of them. But I didn't want to draw attention to them, or to us, by calling out to them.

'We did see one other thing,' said Fang. 'Man, or something in the image of man.'

'It seems to be made of stone,' She-la explained.

'It's standing over there beside the ruins of man's place,' continued Fang. 'Looking out across the bog.'

The old fox, who was enjoying the fruits of the hunt that had been carried out by the younger foxes, licked his lips and grunted. 'I hope he sees the damage man has done to the Fragrant Wood.

'I wonder if he can see any way of getting across?' quipped Young Black Tip.

Fang laughed. 'If he can, he's not telling us!'

Old Sage Brush pushed aside a rabbit bone and licked his lips. 'Has Ratwiddle settled down for the night?'

'As settled as he can be,' said Hop-along. 'And that's not saying much.'

'Don't worry,' Fang assured him, 'I'll keep an eye on him.

'Right then,' said the old fox. 'Perhaps we'll find the answer to our problem if we sleep on it.'

Sleep on it they did, but it was a sleep from which Fang roused them at the first light of dawn. 'It's Ratwiddle,' he panted. 'He's gone off along the edge of the water. I couldn't stop him.'

'What do you think he's up to?' asked Hop-along.

'I don't know,' Fang replied. 'All he kept saying was that he could hear man singing.'

'Singing?' said She-la. 'Well, if he's singing, it isn't the one who's made of stone!'

The young foxes laughed, and then, remembering what his mother had said back in the Land of Sinna, Young Black Tip reminded them, 'That's what Ratwiddle told Vickey, up at the old oak. He told her he could hear man singing. He said "Man is standing on an eel, and he's singing like a cuckoo".'

'Well,' said Old Sage Brush, 'if man's around, we'd better be careful.' He got up and walked to the edge of the bushes. The others were already there, and he asked, 'What's Ratwiddle doing now?' When there was no reply, he asked, 'Can you see him?'

The others hadn't replied to the old fox, because they were speechless. They just couldn't believe what they were seeing.

'I know you won't believe it,' said Twinkle, finding her voice at last. 'But Ratwiddle is walking on the water.'

'You mean, he's swimming?' asked the old fox.

'No, he's not swimming,' She-la told him. 'He's walking on top of it.'

'In fact,' said Fang, 'he's walking all over it.'

'And he's not even looking where he's going,' said Twinkle. 'He's zig-zagging all over the place.'

'He's across now,' said Scat. 'He's on the other side.'

'Has man seen him, do you think?' asked Old Sage Brush.

'Only the one made of stone,' She-la assured him.

'What's he doing now?' asked the old fox.

'Lying down, scratching himself,' said Twinkle.

'He's gone now,' added Fang. 'Up over the hill.'

Young Black Tip trotted down to the edge of the water, saying, 'Maybe if he can do it, so can we.' The others watched, and when he walked in out of his depth, they laughed. Swimming back, he shook the water from his coat. 'I don't understand it,' he said.

'Neither do we,' confessed the old fox. 'But there must be an answer to it.

'Dippers can walk on water,' said Little Running Fox. 'You told us once.'

That was just a figure of speech,' said the old fox. 'What they're really walking on is the stones at the bottom of the river.'

'But there are no stones here,' Young Black Tip pointed out. 'Just mud.'

'No stones here,' repeated the old fox. 'But are there any over there, where Ratwiddle was?'

Making sure there was no one around to see them, they made their way along the edge of the water, trying it now and then with their paws to see if they could locate anything solid.

'Mud,' said Scat.

'Mud,' said Young Black Tip. 'I told you, there's nothing there but mud'.

'Wait a minute,' said Fang. He was farther along, nearer to where he reckoned Ratwiddle had entered the water. 'There's something hard under the surface here. But I can't see whether it's stones or wood.' He walked out a short distance and for a moment he seemed to be walking on the water. Then he dropped out of sight, surfaced and swam back. 'The water's too dark,' he told them. 'I can't see where I'm walking.'

'So there *is* a pathway across the water,' said Old Sage Brush.

'From the way Ratwiddle was going,' Twinkle recalled, 'it must zig-zag all over the place.'

'Perhaps,' She-la suggested, 'it's a secret path, built by man when he lived on the island.'

'Hidden just under the water,' said Hop-along, 'so that his enemies wouldn't find it.'

'Hop-along,' said Old Sage Brush. 'You are slow, but sure-footed. Because man has left you with only three paws, you must probe your way more carefully than any other. Do you think you could find his secret path?'

Hop-along went over to the edge of the water. 'I could try,' he said.

The others watched intently as Hop-along hobbled onto the hidden path. Using his front paw, he probed the peaty water every now and then to make sure he wasn't going to take an empty step. In this way he was able to follow the path, and telling the others to follow him, he slowly led them across to the other side.

'Well done!' said Little Running Fox when they found themselves on dry land. 'I think you should be our path-finder, not me.'

'Look,' whispered She-la.

The others followed her gaze, and found themselves looking up at the man of stone. Above his unseeing eyes he wore a tall pointed hat, and in his hand was a shepherd's crook. But it was what they saw beneath his feet that amazed them.

'He's standing on an eel!' gasped Scat.

At the same time they seemed to hear, as if from afar, the sound of man singing – not with one voice, but with many. The voices rose and fell like the wind, but all the time they were high and soft, like the call of the cuckoo. Then, like the sound of the wind, the singing was gone, and the foxes wondered if they had really heard it, or if they had just been imagining what Ratwiddle had predicted. 'I see man standing on an eel,' he had told Vickey, 'and he's singing like a cuckoo.'

'Lead on,' said Old Sage Brush impatiently. 'It's badgers we came to find, not eels or cuckoos.'

The foxes had no way of knowing that they had now arrived on what was, for man, hallowed ground. Here, long before the rainbow bird had come, long before the Fragrant Wood had even been seeded, man had come to worship a new God. He had built his house on a hill from which he could see his enemies coming, and he had built a secret causeway beneath the water to prevent them stealing his sacred cups. The man of stone who guarded the secret causeway had been built in remembrance of the one who had first come with the message of hope. His enemies had set the giant wolfhound upon him, but somehow he had lived to spread his message and banish the serpent from the land.

The foxes, of course, knew nothing of such things, nor would they have understood it if they had known. What they did know of man gave them little hope that he would ever understand them. If man was standing on an eel today, they knew, he would be standing on a fox or badger tomorrow. If he wasn't destroying their dens and defacing the countryside, he would be devising other ways of getting rid of them. But here, at least, the badgers of the Fragrant Wood had survived, and with the help of the fox they might find a new home.

With a last look back at what remained of the Fragrant Wood, Old Sage Brush and his friends made their way up over the hill and joined the badgers beneath the house where man had once sung his message of hope.

TEN

The Year of the Snipe

A sound that man might have mistaken for the bleating of a goat could be heard in the clear morning air above the ruins of the monastery. But the badgers who were gathered beneath its ancient cloisters knew better. Bad as their eyesight might be, the badgers knew more about the bog that surrounded the Fragrant Wood than man did. And they knew much about the other creatures that lived in it. Unlike the foxes, the badgers rarely went abroad in daylight, and when they did they never lifted their small glassy eyes to see what flew above them. Yet they knew, just as surely as the foxes, did that the bleating sound was coming from the snipe as it swooped above its breeding grounds.

Perhaps the foxes, who had often watched the aerial display of the snipe, could have told the badgers that it produced the bleating sound by spreading its tail and letting the air whirr through the feathers. What neither needed telling was that the bleating or drumming of the snipe was a sure sign that there were nests in the area, and where there were nests there was food. However, all of them knew that in spite of its noisy display, the snipe built a nest that was always well concealed.

Easier to find, they thought, was the nest of the curlew, whose sweet bubbling call now rose and fell somewhere out in the bog. The curlew, they knew, was also rising and falling above its breeding grounds, its long legs sticking out behind it like the heron's. But as always the curlew seemed to be far away, and for the moment it was the call of another bird that was of more immediate concern to the creatures who were gathered in the catacombs beneath the ruins of the monastery. It was the call of the cuckoo.

The cuckoo had also been a source of concern to the monks who had once lived and died in this lonely place. Even though they seldom if ever saw it, it had played an important part in their public prayers and in their private fears.

At some stage man had written of this elusive bird:

In April come he will,
In May he sings all day.
In June he changes his tune
In July he gets ready to fly
And in August go he must . . .

But where was the cuckoo to be found? If anyone set out to search for it, it always fell silent and another took up the call. It was the will-o'-the-wisp of the woods, each new call a distraction. And so the monks, in their search for knowledge, had prayed for the strength to stay on their chosen spiritual path and not be distracted by unimportant things which, like the cuckoo, might mislead them.

There were those who said the monks' songs of praise could still be heard, but their bodies had long since turned to dust, and nothing remained, not even their bones. The slabs in which they had been laid to rest had been toppled by the ravages of time and where there had been order, there was now disarray. The smell of sanctity had gone, and in its place was the musky odour of the badgers. Heaps of well-trodden soil now covered the floor, making mounds where once there had been pieces of marble, for beneath the foundations, the badgers had excavated huge catacombs of their own, converting the burial place of man into a place where they themselves could live.

'I've never seen so many badgers,' Twinkle told Old Sage Brush. 'They're everywhere.'

'And the young ones,' added Scat, 'they're all over the place.'

'I know,' said the old fox. He paused as two young badgers who were chasing each other almost bowled him over. 'I can hear them.'

'I hope they're not expecting us to lead all this lot to a new sett,' said Little Running Fox.

The truth of what the little fox had said was so obvious that none of the others thought it necessary to reply.

Soon after the foxes arrived, the biggest of the badgers called a meeting. His name, they learned, was Musta. The dominant boar in the sett, he could obviously muster a lot of strength. His heavy body reeked with musk from his scent glands, and somehow his name seemed to be very appropriate. However, the real strength in the sett, it soon transpired, was not Musta, but his mate, Meles.

'Musta patrols the boundaries and keeps the young boars in check,' one of the other badgers explained. 'But it's Meles who decides which of us can mate and when.'

The foxes nodded in a gesture that indicated they understood, but in reality they didn't, for as they looked at all the young badgers running around they couldn't help thinking that the older ones must have been mating fairly freely.

'As you can see,' said Meles, almost as if she was reading their thoughts, 'we're a little cramped for space.'

'So I gather,' said the old fox.

'I'm sorry,' Meles hastened to add. 'I had forgotten.' She paused before venturing to ask, 'Is it true what they say – that you are blind?'

'It is true,' the old fox told her. 'I am blind. But that does not mean I cannot see.'

Meles smiled. 'Of course not. Unfortunately, we are the ones who are blind – even though we can see.'

Musta pushed his great bulk up so that he was almost sitting. 'That is why we have asked you to help us'.

As befitting the two who ruled the sett, Musta and Meles were sitting on a mound of earth in the centre of what had once been the floor of the catacomb. Many of the other badgers watched and waited. They were obviously anxious to hear what was going to be said, but despite repeated warnings, the cubs continued to play, wrestling and rolling and chasing one another around.

'Take them outside,' Meles ordered. Immediately boars and sows rounded up their cubs and herded them out of sight. Meles smiled. 'That's better. At least, now we can hear ourselves talk.'

'Does man still live here?' asked Hop-along.

Musta grunted, and told him, 'No, why do you ask?'

'It's just that we thought we . . .' She-la hesitated and looked at Ratwiddle, who was sitting nearby scratching himself. 'We thought we heard him singing.'

Ratwiddle stopped scratching and said, 'Man sings like the cuckoo.'

Musta looked at Ratwiddle for a moment, as if he couldn't quite figure him out. 'When the wind blows through the stones above us,' he told them, 'we can hear many things.'

'You asked us for guidance,' said Old Sage Brush, bringing them all back down to earth. 'What is it you require of us?'

'We want you to lead us to the Fragrant Wood,' Meles told them.

Fang, who had been silent for a long time, asked, 'You mean, all of you?'

Musta shook his head. 'Of course not. Just a few.'

'But I thought you had come here when the Fragrant Wood was destroyed,' said Hop-along.

Musta nodded.

'So we did.' Realising that they didn't understand, he eased his huge bulk onto the flattened soil, saying, 'How can I explain it?'

Meles looked at him. 'Perhaps I should do it.' Shuffling closer to the foxes, she told them, 'You see, the wise ones of our setts have always had a saying. It's a saying that gives us reassurance when we are cubs and comfort when we have cubs of our own . . . '

The foxes listened in silence as she went on to recite:

The sweetest bird on the branches singing,
The cuckoo on top of the green hill;
And death shall never find us
In the bosom of the fragrant wood.

'They were right,' said Little Running Fox. 'Death hasn't found you. But your fragrant wood has been destroyed.'

'True,' said Musta. 'This one has been destroyed. But, as you say, death has not found all of us and the wise ones tell us that we must be strong in our resolve to find a new home.'

'We must not be misled by the cuckoo,' added Meles. 'We must search out the green hill where things grow in abundance and the cuckoo is at rest.'

Old Sage Brush nodded. 'So you believe there is another Fragrant Wood out there somewhere?'

'We know there is,' Musta told him. 'We also know how to get there. The problem is, we cannot do it on our own.'

'Why not?' asked Fang.

'Well,' Meles explained, 'we know from the word that has been passed on from one sett to another where it is. But what we do not know is how to cross man's pathways to get to it. His machines have killed many of us, and not one, as far as we know, has succeeded in reaching it, at least, not from this part of the world.'

'We too have lost many lives trying to cross man's pathways,' said She-la. 'Especially young foxes striking out on their own.'

'Nevertheless,' insisted Meles, 'your hearing is good, and your eyes are better. Much better than ours.' She turned to Old Sage Brush. 'And even though you cannot see at all, you are very wise. Otherwise you would not have found your way here.'

'What exactly do you want us to do?' asked Hop-along.

'We want you to take some of our young,' said Musta, 'and guide them to the Fragrant Wood.'

'We would never be able to control them,' said Scat.

'Their parents will go with them,' said Meles. 'All you have to do is guide them.'

'How many?' asked Fang.

'Three families,' said Musta. 'Three should be enough'.

The foxes knew that what Musta was really saying was that three families should be enough to ensure that some of them at least would get through, but they said nothing.

Then Old Sage Brush, who had remained silent for most of the conversation, cleared his throat. 'But there is something you have not told us.' He paused and the others waited to hear what it was. 'I was given to understand that the place you seek lies in the Valley of the Dragon.'

'Who among us has ever seen a dragon?' asked Musta. 'Certainly no badger ever has.' He took a deep breath through his nose. 'But then our eyesight is not as good as yours.'

Old Sage Brush smiled. 'I know of no fox who has seen one either.' He paused before adding, 'Except, of course, our friend, Ratwiddle.'

They all looked at Ratwiddle, who seemed to be eyeing the ruins above him with one eye. 'I see many dragons,' he told them. 'They are spitting fire at the mountain and man is running to the earth.' He started to scratch himself, then stopped to add, 'And I see flames running to the sky.'

The other foxes, of course, were accustomed to Ratwiddle's predictions, and while they didn't understand them, they weren't surprised. The badgers, on the other hand, were visibly shocked, and Meles asked, 'What does your friend mean?'

'Who knows,' said Old Sage Brush. 'He himself will tell you his mind is full of dragons.'

'You can't kill dragons, you know,' Ratwiddle added, and getting to his feet, he disappeared into the shadows.

'It's the rats,' explained She-la. 'He's always hunting them.'

'And they've done strange things to his mind,' said Hop-along.

'Nevertheless,' said Old Sage Brush, 'there is always a grain of truth in what he says. So be warned. This journey will not be without its dangers.'

'Life is full of dangers,' Musta replied, 'as you well know. And for us the greatest danger is to do nothing.

'Very well,' said the old fox. 'But there is also danger in numbers, so we will have to split up.'

'When do you propose to leave?' asked Meles.

'In the morning,' replied the old fox. 'We will leave on the wings of the morning'.

A soft breeze was blowing across the bog, and when the foxes went outside they found it very refreshing after the mustiness of the meeting with the badgers. Some of the badgers, they could see, were now snuffling around, looking for worms. Somehow the foxes felt like something more substantial, but when Fang and Young Black Tip scouted around, they reported that there was little of substance to be found, so they all settled down and waited for the dawn.

Soon the older foxes were asleep, but the younger ones were fascinated by what was going on around them. Their long black ears twitched to the playful sounds of the young badgers, and their eyes turned to every move they made. Growing out of the side of the ruins, they could see, was an old ash tree. Its roots were clasped around the stones and it had several trunks, all of which were now being used as scratching posts by some of the badger cubs. Other cubs were frolicking down at the water's edge, and they seemed to like the water, something that surprised the foxes, for they had never seen badgers taking to the water before. The younger foxes were also surprised to see how quickly the badgers could run, and all of this pleased them, as they knew it would make the task that lay ahead of them much easier.

After a while the badger cubs complied, though somewhat reluctantly, with their parents' command to return to the sett. Peace and quiet spread across the small island and the young foxes lay and listened to the wind. Eventually they dozed, and as they did so, they once again thought they heard the sound of singing coming from the ruins. It was the sound of man, or so it seemed, but it was a sound that carried no threat, and soon they drifted off to sleep.

If it was the sound of man the young foxes heard, it was a sound from the past, a sound from the time when man, in his search for knowledge, had prayed to his God to preserve him from the cuckoo.

Of these lofty things, the foxes who now sheltered beside the monastery knew nothing. All they knew was that they too would have to stay on their chosen path, and with a number of young badgers in tow, it wouldn't be easy. It wasn't the cuckoo, but the drumming of the snipe that awakened them, and when they listened to the wind whirring through its tail feathers in the early dawn, they knew the wings of the morning had arrived. It was time to be on their way.

ELEVEN

The Year of the Fox

There was a touch of early-morning mist in the air around the monastery, and had man been up and about he would have seen the snipe that rose above it, but not the creatures who waited to cross the path that lay just below the water.

Musta and Meles had proposed that the foxes should take just three families of badgers, but She-la was still worried. 'There will be too many of us,' she protested. 'We will leave a trail that even a . . .'

Old Sage Brush smiled. '. . . That even a blind fox could follow?'

'Well, yes – no, I didn't mean that.'

Sensing that She-la was flustered by what he had said, Old Sage Brush assured her, 'I know what you mean, and you're quite right. We would leave a trail that many of our enemies could see with their eyes closed. But, as I said last night, it is not my intention that we should all travel together. We will have to split up, and as there are three families of badgers, I think it is only natural that we should split into three groups.

'But that will pose other dangers for us,' said She-la. 'Some of us, like Hop-along, will be more exposed.'

Old Sage Brush nodded. 'I know. But the strong can help the weak, and the weak can always be a source of strength to the strong'.

'How will we split up then?' asked Hop-along.

Old Sage Brush thought for a moment before saying, 'I think Young Black Tip should go with you and She-la.'

'I don't wish to be troublesome,' said She-la, 'but would it not be more natural for Scat to come with us?'

'It probably would,' the old fox agreed. 'But even though he is now a mature young fox, he is still your cub, and instead of helping each other, you would be telling him what to do. No, I think it is better that Young Black Tip should go with you.'

Hop-along nodded. 'I suppose you're right. So who will Scat go with?'

'With Fang. Twinkle and Little Running Fox can come with me.'

The young foxes nodded, and Fang said, 'But you're forgetting Ratwiddle.'

Old Sage Brush smiled. 'No one can tell Ratwiddle who he should travel with. He will go where his mind takes him and hopefully he will choose to follow one of our groups.'

'Tell me, old fox,' said Meles, as they prepared to leave, 'why did you agree to come and help us?'

Old Sage Brush paused and turned in her direction. 'Why did you decide to ask me?'

Meles smiled. 'Because we knew you'd come.'

'But you still haven't answered our question,' said Musta. 'Why *did* you come?'

Old Sage Brush shrugged. 'For the same reason you knew I *would* come.'

Musta and Meles nodded their striped heads as if to say they understood, but the younger foxes didn't understand, and later, when Scat asked the old fox what he had meant, he just said, 'There's more to life than hanging around an oak tree like a bat waiting for the dark.'

Scat was still puzzled, and before they split up into different groups, he asked his mother what the old fox had meant.

'Maybe,' said She-la, 'he means he's not going to hang around waiting to die.'

'And maybe,' suggested Hop-along, 'he doesn't like the idea of the badgers having to do the same.'

Whatever he meant, Old Sage Brush decided that they shouldn't hang around the monastery any longer than necessary. Watched by striped heads from numerous holes in the island, Hop-along led the three groups across the hidden causeway, one by one, and by the time the sun had burned the mist from the water they had reached the lower slopes of the mountain.

Harebell was as good as her word, and was waiting for them with some of her friends in a hidden hollow just below the mountain.

'What about the wolfhounds?' asked Fang. 'Are they still on the other side?'

'We haven't seen them for a day or two,' Harebell told them. 'But they're over there somewhere.'

'They've probably found something else to chase,' said Bindweed.

'As soon as we get to the other side,' Fang told them, 'each group will have to go its own way. We'll just have to hope that the wolfhounds don't find any of us again.'

'But how can we cross the mountain without them seeing us?' asked Twinkle.

'I think it's too dangerous to go back the way we came,' said Harebell. 'The badger cubs are very young, and some of the ledges are very narrow. Perhaps it might be better if we took you around the mountain. It will take us longer, but it will be a lot safer and we may also be able to avoid the wolfhounds.'

She-la looked at her mate and at Old Sage Brush. Both were resting now after the steep climb, and the thought of taking a route that would make their journey longer was the last thing she wanted. However, she knew Harebell was right. The young badgers, she was glad to see, ran fast between their parents, but they ran blindly, and might not survive the narrow mountain paths. Perhaps if they could all rest until darkness, Old Sage Brush and Hop-along would be ready for the longer journey around the mountain, and it might be safer for them too, especially if the wolfhounds were still running around on the other side. 'What do you think?' she asked Harebell. 'Could you find your way around the mountain in the dark?'

Harebell smiled. 'To take the short-cut across the mountain we must travel by day. But if we travel around it, we do not need the light.'

'And anyway,' said Primrose, 'the mountain is never truly in the dark, especially when the wide eye is above it to show us the way.'

She-la nodded. 'The wide eye of gloomglow.'

Accustomed to sleeping during the day, and obviously tired from running so far, most of the badgers had snuggled into one another at the base of a massive boulder and were fast asleep. Only two of the adults were awake, and now and then one of them would trot up the slope to the edge of the hollow and scan the far side. Seeing that they were worried about something, She-la asked Fang to go over and find out what it was.

'It's the wolfhounds,' the boar badger admitted when Fang brought them over. 'We have heard many stories about them, and now that we are on the mountain the thought of them agitates us greatly.'

'But it is on the other side of the mountain that they hunt,' Harebell assured them. 'Not here.'

The sow badger lifted her long striped nose to scent the wind and said, 'Nevertheless, the giant hounds hunt somewhere in our path, and we cannot hope to outrun them. Our legs are too short.'

Scat stepped forward and pushed out his chest. 'I outran them and my legs are not much longer than yours.'

The other foxes looked at Scat and smiled. He had greatly improved in both body and spirit since they had set out on their journey, but he was still a very scrawny little fox.

The boar badger looked at Old Sage Brush, who was still sleeping, and said, 'But your wise one would say it took more than legs to outrun the giant hounds. Your eyes and ears are very sharp and you have a certain . . .' He paused as if wondering whether to use the word: '. . . a certain cunning that we do not have.'

'If it was our cunning that helped us,' Twinkle told them, 'then it will help you. That is why we came to guide you.'

The two badgers nodded.

'But here we are talking to you,' said She-la, anxious to change the subject, 'and we don't even know your names.'

'Sorry, my name is Musteli,' said the boar badger.

'And my name is Meles Meles,' added the sow.

'But isn't that the same name as . . . ' Little Running Fox paused, not wishing to appear stupid.

'As our elders?' The sow badger shook her head. 'No, no. They are Musta and Meles. We are Musteli and Meles Meles. Our cubs are . . .'

'Don't tell me,' said Fang. 'Meles Meles Meles.'

The sow badger smiled. 'Something like that.'

'It all sounds very complicated,' said Scat.

The boar badger nodded. 'I suppose it does. But it poses no difficulty for us.'

'It's been done that way in our setts for generations,' his mate explained. 'By using these name patterns we always know who is who and who our relatives are.'

Harebell, who had listened to all this with great interest, cocked her head so that she could look at the badgers with one of her big brown eyes, and said, 'But I always assumed that badgers who lived in a wood would be called after the trees. You know, the way we are called after the flowers.'

The sow badger smiled. 'I am sure there is a flower for every hare, but I'm afraid there are more of us than there are trees.'

'We have often looked down at the wood and wondered about you,' said Dandelion. 'Where did you live?'

'We lived on the outskirts, not far from the bog,' the sow badger told her. 'Our sett was beneath the alders and the hazel.'

'There you are then,' said Harebell. 'Why don't we call you Alder and Hazel?'

The boar looked at his mate as if to see how the name Hazel might fit. 'Mmm. Why not? Yes, I think Hazel's a lovely name.'

Taking this remark as the compliment it was intended to be, the sow badger smiled. 'But what about the rules of our sett . . . the tradition?'

'When we reach our destination,' her mate told her, 'we'll have our own sett. We'll make our own rules.'

The sow badger smiled again. 'All right then. Alder it is. And I must say I think it suits you very well.'

'You mean,' said another voice, '*if* we reach our destination.'

They looked around to see that one of the other adult badgers had trotted over to join them.

'Surely,' said yet another voice, 'whatever lies ahead of you is preferable to what you leave behind.'

'Sage Brush,' said Young Black Tip. 'We thought you were asleep.'

The old fox chuckled. 'Didn't you know that a blind fox can sleep with one eye open?' He chuckled again, and added, 'One ear too.'

TWELVE

The Year of Man

It was coming on to evening now and, while it was still bright, empty stomachs were obviously telling the young badgers it was time to eat.

'Better tell them to keep out of sight,' cautioned Harebell. 'Just in case.'

'You mean, in case of the wolfhounds?' asked one of the adult badgers.

Harebell shook her head. 'There are sheep in the foothills and where there are sheep there is danger. Sometimes man and his dogs come up to check on them, so be careful.'

'Tell me, Alder,' said Old Sage Brush, giving his seal of approval to what he had overheard, 'why did man destroy your setts? Was it because of his cows?'

'This is not cow country,' the badger told him. 'If you could see you would know that the only pasture is here in the foothills of the mountain and that is for sheep. The rest, at least as far as our territory went, was wood, scrub and bog.'

Hop-along hobbled over to join them and settled down beside She-la.

'We had lived in the wood for longer than anyone could remember,' said Hazel. 'And in all that time man had never bothered us. Every generation of badgers added new tunnels to the setts and they ran in every direction and at different levels throughout the entire wood.'

'You could go into a sett at one side of the wood,' Alder explained, 'and come out at the other side.'

'Or you could come up at any tree or any place you wanted,' continued Hazel, 'the network was so extensive, the entrance holes so numerous. The only sounds we ever heard came from the trees above us, which were full of birds, and no one ever came near us, except maybe a magpie that was curious to see if we were in or wanted to show his friends how brave he was.'

'There was plenty of food for everyone,' said Alder. 'We shared the grubs of the wood with the birds, and the nuts of the trees with the squirrels, and when we felt like a change we hunted frogs in the streams at the edge of the bog.'

'The bog also helped to keep our young from straying too far away,' said Hazel. 'The bog-holes are dangerous, and from an early age they knew not to go there on their own.'

'We lived on the edge of the bog,' said one of the other adult badgers. 'Or the edge of the wood, whichever way you look at it. That's why we escaped.'

'Our sett was under the brambles,' explained his mate. 'It was the blackberries that gave us our change of food.'

'Most of us who escaped lived near the edge,' confirmed Hazel. 'Our other two friends lived under the ash trees and the silver birch.'

'But what happened?' asked She-la. 'What happened to bring it all to such a terrible end?'

'One day,' Hazel recalled, 'we heard a dreadful high-pitched sound, and when we looked out we saw man cutting down the trees.'

'We were afraid,' said Alder, 'but we sat tight, hoping, I suppose, that the danger might go away.'

'But it didn't,' Hazel recalled. 'When man had cut down the trees he brought in huge machines to tear up the roots. In doing that he tore our setts asunder and buried many of our friends alive.'

'Were they not able to dig their way out?' asked Hop-along.

'Some of them did,' said Alder, 'and when night came, and the machines fell silent, we went back to help them. But the upheaval of rocks and roots was too great. We found more dead bodies than survivors.'

'And of course,' Hazel added, 'many of the dead were cubs.'

The thought of such a tragedy produced an uncomfortable silence that was broken only by the sounds of the badger cubs as they searched among the sheep droppings for grubs.

Later, as they waited for the moon to appear in the sky, Hazel slipped away from her own kind and sought out Harebell.

'In a way,' Hazel whispered, 'I can understand the fox helping the badger. But the hare helping the fox, that is something I cannot understand.'

Harebell tilted her head to one side so that one of her big brown eyes could see if there was any sign of what they called the wide eye of gloomglow, and told her, 'I suppose it must seem strange all right. But, to tell you the truth, it's because of the one with the black tip that I decided to help them.'

'How come?' asked Hazel.

'Well,' Harebell confided, 'it wasn't always the giant hounds that I had to contend with. Once, when I was young, many mountain hares – nearly all of us, in fact – were rounded up and caught by man. He set the gaze-hounds on us and many were killed. I would have been killed too, but for the fact that two young foxes showed us how we could escape. Somehow I suspect they were intrigued by the sight of so many hares gathered in one place and wanted to release us so they could chase us themselves. Anyway, as it so happened, I was the only one to get away. I made it back to the mountain, and I will never forget the foxes who helped us, especially the one with the black tip on his tail.'

'Do you think that fox was Young Black Tip?' asked Hazel.

Harebell shrugged. 'Who knows? But it was really because the foxes showed me how to escape from the gazehounds that I showed them how to escape from the wolfhounds.'

'And if they hadn't escaped from the wolfhounds,' said Hazel, 'they wouldn't have been able to help us escape from the island.'

Harebell was about to remind Hazel that the danger wasn't over yet, when someone else with his head cocked to one side ran up out of the hollow. While they had been talking, the soft light of gloomglow had crept across the foothills unnoticed. Unnoticed, that is, by all except Ratwiddle, and he was now on his way.

Only the curious eyes of the mountain sheep noticed the strange mixture of shadowy figures slipping silently through the foothills. Dandelion led the way, stopping now and then on top of a hill to see if the way was clear and to ensure that Ratwiddle and those who followed wouldn't run into any trouble. The others had split up into groups led by Harebell, Primrose and Bindweed, and the hares made sure there was enough distance between the groups so that if danger did arise, some of them at least could get away. But man and his dogs were asleep and far from the mountain as this strange alliance of badger, fox and hare made their way around it, and before the sun had burned away the early morning mist, they had settled safely into a secluded field on the other side.

Whatever about the badgers, the foxes had felt very exposed on the bare slopes of the mountain, and even though they knew they might be nearer the wolfhounds now, they were relieved to be back in the fields whose ditches and hedges were more familiar to them. As they rested, Old Sage Brush heard the birds singing in the hedgerows and asked Scat to tell him what he saw.

'There's cuckoo spit on the vetch,' Scat told him. 'And on the goosegrass. The docks are tall and green and there's some cuckoo spit on them as well.' Looking up at the hedgerows, he went on, 'The elderberry and the hogweed are in bloom, but the blossoms have gone from the hawthorn and in their place are small green haws.'

'Ah, I remember,' said the old fox. 'Green, but with a tinge of crimson. And what about the blackthorn?'

'The sloes are a bit bigger,' Scat replied, 'almost as big as rabbit droppings. But they're still green too.'

The sun was gaining strength now, and feeling its heat on his back, the old fox asked, just as he had asked when they had left the Land of the Rainbow Bird, 'And what about the rose? Has the summer rose come upon the briar?'

Scat nodded. 'Some. They're white, or is it pink? I'm not sure.'

Twinkle, who was lying nearby, looked up at the long sweeping briars. Somehow, she thought, the roses looked almost too delicate to sit upon such great hooked thorns. 'Isn't it strange,' she said. 'I have seen man picking the flowers of the fields, but never the summer rose.'

'Perhaps man has learned something you already know,' said the old fox.

'What's that?' asked Scat.

'Maybe he has learned that you can't lick honey from a briar.' Old Sage Brush struggled to his feet. 'Now, take me over to Harebell. Before we take our leave, there are one or two things I should like to know myself.'

Wondering what the old fox meant, Scat and Twinkle guided him over to where Harebell was resting in a clump of long grass.

'Tell me, Harebell,' he said, after he had eased himself down beside her. 'How is it that we have seen no jack hares on the mountain?'

'For a fox that is blind,' Harebell replied, 'you see a lot'.

'I may be blind,' said the old fox, 'but I am not stupid.'

Harebell paused, wondering how she should reply. 'The jack hares are there all right,' she said. 'They're guarding our young.'

'Who from?' asked Old Sage Brush. 'Surely not from us?'

If a wry smile crossed Harebell's face, the old fox couldn't see it. 'Let's say,' she said, 'they're guarding them from the wolfhounds.

If the old fox detected the slightest hint of distrust in her voice, he didn't show it. Instead, he said, 'Speaking of the giant hounds, you never did tell us how you managed to outrun them – or us, for that matter'.

'If you were a hare, and I was a fox,' said Harebell, 'would you tell me the secret of your survival?'

Old Sage Brush smiled. 'You know, Harebell,' he said, 'with cunning like that, you should have been a fox'.

The sun was up now and it was time to go. Having thanked the hares for their help, Old Sage Brush organised the badgers into three groups again. By this time the adult badgers had accepted their new names and readily responded to the old fox's directions. 'Alder and Hazel, you take your three cubs and go with

Young Black Tip, Hop-along and She-la. Birch and Ash, you and your cubs – two, isn't it? – you go with Fang and Scat. That leaves Bramble and Blackberry.'

'We also have two cubs,' said Blackberry.

Old Sage Brush nodded. 'Fine, you come with Little Running Fox, Twinkle, and myself.'

Harebell hopped over to the old fox. 'And what about Ratwiddle? Who will he go with?'

'He'll go with whoever he pleases,' the old fox told her.

Ash shuffled over and said to Harebell, 'Forgive me for asking, but the thought of the giant hounds worries us greatly. Do you think it is likely that we will encounter them?'

Harebell was sitting upright now, her long ears erect and alert. 'It is not my wish to alarm you unduly,' she replied, 'and I do wish you a safe journey to your new home.' She looked around as if the thought of the wolfhounds had suddenly made her nervous. 'But it will be difficult for all of you to slip past them unnoticed.'

The others couldn't help but hear this, and She-la said, 'You mean, they're likely to pick up the trail of one of our groups?'

When Harebell nodded, Blackberry added, 'So the question is, which one?'

'Don't worry,' said Fang. 'We've outrun the giant hounds before. We can do it again.'

But if Fang was trying to reassure the badgers, the familiar voice of Ratwiddle chipped in to say, 'You can't outrun the dragons, or the flames that run to the sky'

The faraway, yet matter-of-fact tone of Ratwiddle's voice sent a shiver through many of those who heard him, and all remained silent, except one of the badgers.

'All that matters,' said Birch in an equally matter-of-fact but determined tone, 'is that some of us outrun them'.

Sensing that all this talk was unnerving both foxes and badgers, Old Sage Brush spoke up to say, 'What we must outrun are the fears that can set our minds on fire. And we won't outrun anything if we stand around here all day talking.'

'And whatever happens,' Alder reminded them, 'we must not let the cuckoo deflect us from our path.' Turning to the other badgers, he told them, 'Always remember what Meles said before we left. We must search out the green hill where things grow in abundance and the cuckoo is at rest.'

With these words they split up, the three groups going their separate ways, but in roughly the same direction. At the same time, the hares bounded away to the mountain and when they were high enough up they stopped to look back. Turning their heads this way and that, they scanned the fields. However, their friends had melted into the surrounding countryside. They turned to go and as they did so, the soft call of the cuckoo drifted up from the fields . . .

THIRTEEN

The Year of the Rat

Having heard their elders talk of the cuckoo many times, and not having understood what they meant, the young badgers had come to regard this bird they had heard but never seen in the same way that man might imagine the call of a vixen to be the cry of a banshee. Now its haunting call seemed to be very close, closer than when they had been in a larger group, and fearing that it had come to stalk them, the three cubs belonging to Alder and Hazel kept their small pointed heads well down and ran, head-to-tail, for all they were worth between their parents.

For his part, Young Black Tip was more concerned with what his eyes and nose told him, and ignoring the call of the cuckoo, he pressed ahead until they reached the safety of a scrub-covered hill. There, as they rested, he suggested that when they resumed their journey, Hop-along should lead the badgers, while he and Shela should keep some distance on either side of them. 'That way,' he explained, 'we'll be able to keep an eye out for the wolfhounds and pick up some food as we go along.'

Hop-along nodded. 'Seems a good idea to me.'

She-la smiled. 'Me too.' In fact, she thought, it was a plan that was worthy of Old Sage Brush himself. For by leading the badgers, Hop-along would see himself as the leader of the group, and yet it was the position in which he would be afforded most protection.

If Hop-along was aware of what was being done for him, he didn't say, but as they continued their journey it became obvious that he was enjoying his new role. Because he was taking the lead, he was able to stop every now and then in the pretence that he was taking stock of the situation, whereas in reality he was taking a rest. He was also able to call a halt when he thought She-la and Young Black Tip should hunt. In such ways, he was able to control the pace of his group while appearing to be in full command of it.

Eventually, however, it began to dawn on Hop-along that, as leader, much more would be expected of him. In particular, the badgers would be looking to him to find a safe way across man's pathways. She-la and Young Black Tip could help him, of course, just as they had done on the way to the mountain. But now, as leader, he would be expected to do it on his own. An animal with a good turn of speed, he reckoned, had some chance of getting across the pathways safely. Speed, though, was not one of his strong points. Looking at the space where his fourth paw should be, he knew he wouldn't be able to go much faster than a hedgehog, and he was all too aware of what happened to the hedgehogs when they ventured across those pathways.

Hoping that he would think of something, Hop-along pressed on. Their progress was slow, and with every faltering step he wondered how he was going to solve the problem. He was still wondering when they arrived at the first of man's pathways, and not knowing what to do, he told the others, 'Wait here. I'll see if there's any way we can get across.'

Anxiously She-la and Young Black Tip watched Hop-along pull himself up the embankment by his one front paw. Their hearts went out to him and their natural inclination was to help him. In the event, neither did so. They knew that such a move would not only hurt his feelings but damage the badgers' faith in his leadership. So they said nothing, and when he whispered back at them, 'Better keep out of sight,' they led the badgers into the safety of the hedge that ran alongside the road.

The truth was, Hop-along didn't want the others to see that he still had no idea how he was going to find a safe way across. It was quite a narrow pathway, he could see, the type that twisted through the country-side like an eel, and for a moment he toyed with the idea that a quick hobble across might be the answer. Then he saw, to his dismay, the body of a fox, or what remained of it, not far from where he stood, and he knew it had been killed by one of man's machines. Instinctively, he took a timorous step towards the pathetic patch of reddish brown, only to see a fat grey rat race up out of the grass verge to feed upon it.

In a surge of anger, Hop-along threw himself along the side of the road towards the rat, all thoughts of safety forgotten. He was almost upon it, when the rat turned and dashed back into the grass. At the same time he heard one of man's machines as it came hurtling around the corner. Startled, he looked up to see the monster bearing down on him, and had barely time to pull himself away from it before it went thundering past. He could feel the passing wind pulling his coat after it and knew he had escaped death by a hair's breadth.

'Are you all right, Hop-along?' It was the anxious voice of She-la calling from the hedge below.

'Of course I am,' he replied. In fact he was trembling with fright and was hoping the others wouldn't hear it in his voice. He was also more annoyed than before and threw himself down the embankment in pursuit of the rat. From the path that was worn in the grass he knew it wasn't the first time the rat had been up to the dead fox. He also knew that as long as there was food there, the rat wouldn't be far away.

He was now a short distance down the hedgerow from the others, and as he made his way along the bottom of it, he heard a rustle that told him the rat was scurrying away through the long grass. Hurrying after it as fast as his front paw could take him, he found to his surprise that it had run into an underground water pipe. In he went, and when he emerged from the other end, he cornered the rat in a drain. Never before had he taken such pleasure in shaking the life out of one of these creatures, and he was carrying it back through the water pipe when he realised that the pipe ran under the road.

A smile came over Hop-along's face, and it wasn't because of the fact that he had caught the rat. When he returned to the others he told them something that was, strictly speaking, true. Dropping the rat at their feet, he said, 'There's no way we can get over man's path with safety. One of our kind has tried, but failed. His body lies up there for the crows to pick and the rats to steal.

'But our path lies beyond that of man,' said Hazel. 'We must find some way to get over it.'

'Perhaps,' replied Hop-along, and Young Black Tip got the distinct impression that he was trying to sound as wise as Old Sage Brush, 'perhaps there is another way.'

'How do you mean, another way?' asked Alder.

'I mean,' Hop-along explained, 'that if you cannot get over an obstacle, and you cannot get around it, then you must try to get under it.'

'Of course,' said She-la. 'When we want to get into a hen-run, we know we cannot get over the fence, so we go under it.'

Hop-along, who was still shaking from his brush with death, told them, 'Precisely.' He then directed his mate to go down the hedgerow one way, Young Black Tip the other, and see what they could find.

When, a short time later, She-la returned to say she had found a water pipe that would take them under man's pathway, the badgers were delighted. They had, they admitted, learned their first lesson from the foxes. She-la and Young Black Tip were delighted too.

Somehow they had a suspicion that Hop-along wasn't telling them everything, but when he picked up the rat and led the way through the pipe to the other side of the road, they were happy to follow him.

In the days and nights that followed they made good progress, Alder and Hazel consulting every now and then with badgers they met to make sure they were still going in the right direction. The young badgers were thriving. In between journeys they slept a lot, ate a lot and, to the frustration of their parents, played a lot, but the family never failed to rejoin the foxes before the morning mist had cleared.

By this time all thoughts of the wolfhounds had been forgotten, and it was only when She-la reported that a dog had picked up their trail that fears of the giant hounds came flooding back into their minds. 'No, it's not the wolfhounds,' she assured them. 'It's a sheepdog.'

'What's it doing?' asked Hop-along.

'I'm not quite sure,' said She-la. 'I think it's stalking us.'

'How do you mean?' asked Young Black Tip.

'It's keeping low. You know, the way they do when they're following sheep.'

'Well, we're not sheep,' asserted Hazel, 'and we're not going to be put off by a sheepdog.'

As it turned out, this was easier said than done. Because the dog continued to skulk around their left flank, they found themselves veering to the right. The foxes weren't unduly concerned at first, but the badgers, mindful of the warnings they had received about the cuckoo, were worried that they might be deflected from their path.

'Let's sweep around it, then, until we get back on track,' suggested Young Black Tip.

The others agreed, but once again this turned out to be easier said than done. Taking off as fast as they could, they were veering back to their original path when they found the sheepdog had moved up alongside them, and they were forced to veer away again.

'Perhaps,' suggested Alder, 'if we circled back we could lose the dog, or at least get on the far side of it.'

This seemed a good idea, but when they tried to break away they found themselves hemmed in by a second sheep dog who had been stalking them on the other side. To their dismay they realised that they were being herded like sheep and driven in a direction they did not want to go.

Finding refuge in an abandoned badger sett, they lay down to get their breath back and consider their situation.

'Maybe they're trying to drive us off their land,' suggested Hazel.

Hop-along nodded. 'If that's all they're trying to do, we'll be all right. But what if they're trying to drive us into danger?'

'You mean, shooters?' asked She-la.

Her mate shrugged. 'I don't know. Could be.'

'What if we continued by night?' suggested Young Black Tip. 'The dogs wouldn't be able to follow us.'

Alder shook his head. 'I don't know. Our sight isn't good.'

'But you forage for food at night,' said Young Black Tip. 'And you take your young out to play at night.'

'That is at our setts,' Hazel reminded him, 'where everything is familiar to us. Out here, in a strange land, we would never find our way in the dark.'

'Then let me show you the way,' said the young fox. 'We know the general direction we want to go, and somehow this land is familiar to me. I have been over it before.'

Hazel looked at Alder and Alder looked at Hop-along. None of them could come up with a better idea, so after a moment's reflection, Alder nodded. 'All right. We'll give it a try.'

Dusk came, and still the small group sat tight. Even the badger cubs accepted the fact that they wouldn't be going out to eat, let alone play. Somewhere out there, they sensed, was danger, and for once they were content to do their parents' bidding. As they waited for the right time to move, Alder and Hazel explored the sett, and when they decided to go, the two badgers led the way through a maze of tunnels until they came to a small opening some distance from the main entrance. 'Now,' Alder whispered to Young Black Tip. 'It's up to you.'

The sounds of man and his animals, which were so intrusive in the light of day, had long since died down. Young Black Tip raised his head into the night so that his long ears and sensitive nose could read the wind. If the sheepdogs were still there, he reckoned, they hadn't heard them. Without a word he led the others down the hedgerow, and when they had reached the safety of the adjoining field, they set off as fast as they could, each following the dark outline of the one in front.

It wasn't long before they had put what they considered a safe distance between themselves and the dogs, and while they still had the cover of darkness, they settled into another badger sett.

'I was hoping we might find a sett that was occupied,' said Hazel.

Alder nodded. He knew his mate liked to mix with her own kind and assure herself that all was well. Had she known what was going through Young Black Tip's mind, she would not have felt at all reassured. Nor, for that matter, would Hop-along or She-la.

Familiar as the fields were to Young Black Tip, it was only when he took stock of the sett they were in that he realised where they were. It also explained why the setts were empty. Unwittingly, he had led his group to the sett where he and the other foxes had stopped on their way to the mountain. His heart sank, for he knew that in spite of his efforts, the sheepdogs had herded them into the area where man had exterminated the badgers. Afraid to say anything, he crept up to the entrance and looked outside. An early morning mist had settled on the field, obscuring his view, but the sounds he heard confirmed his worst fears. Man was there, and so were his dogs.

A quick check of all the entrances and exits told Young Black Tip that they were surrounded. By this time, the others could see that something was wrong, and when he told them what was happening, a great fear gripped them. She-la feared for Hop-along, Alder and Hazel feared for their young, and having led them there, Young Black Tip feared for them all.

'What do you think they're going to do?' asked Alder.

Young Black Tip shook his head. 'I don't know. But I think they're waiting for the mist to clear before they move.'

Hop-along struggled to his feet. 'Then we must move before they do.'

'Do you mean, make a run for it?' asked Hazel.

Young Black Tip looked at She-la, then at her mate. 'We'd never make it,' he said.

'Maybe not all of us,' said Hop-along. 'But some of us might.'

'Perhaps,' suggested Young Black Tip, 'if I drew them off.'

Hop-along hobbled up to the entrance and, from the darkness of the sett, looked out. A very low mist still covered the field, and beneath it he could see one of the dogs, the rubber boots of a man and the end of a gun. Beyond them were some sheep, heads raised as they wondered what was going on. If the rat could find a way under man's pathway, he thought, then maybe, just maybe, they could find a way out under man's very nose. Rejoining the others, he said, 'All right, we'll make a run for it. But we must go before the mist lifts.'

She-la agreed and, turning to Young Black Tip, told him, 'Earlier on our journey you suggested that we travel in a way that has served us well – Hop-along and the badgers in the centre, you and I on the outside. If we stick to that, it may serve us well again.'

'In what way?' asked Alder, who, like his mate, had no knowledge of such cunning.

'Well,' said She-la, 'if Young Black Tip goes one way and I go the other, Hop-along and yourselves just might be able to slip away through the middle.'

'But that will be very dangerous for you and Young Black Tip,' said Hazel.

'Dangerous, yes,' replied She-la, 'but we are all in danger, and if we don't do something we will all die.'

Young Black Tip moved towards the entrance and braced himself. 'Right then,' he said. 'The sooner we go the better.'

Without another word he bounded out of the sett. Startled, someone fired a shot. A dog barked and sheep bleated. She-la bolted and there was another shot. In the confusion, someone shouted, 'Watch you don't shoot the dogs.' 'Or the sheep,' someone else added.

The dogs, Hop-along could see, had gone after Young Black Tip, the shooters after She-la. Seizing his chance, he led the badgers straight out under the mist. Soon they were in among the sheep who, in their confusion, moved with them across the field, and almost before they knew it they had reached the safety of the far hedge.

With the mist so low to the ground, the shooters had no hope of seeing She-la again. The two sheep-dogs, on the other hand, were underneath the mist.

They could see just as well as the foxes, and were now hard on the heels of Young Black Tip. Not knowing where he was going or what he was going to do, the young fox ran for all he was worth. Using the cover of drains and hedges, he kept going until he found himself at a farmyard. There he stopped and looked back. In spite of the mist, the two dogs had gained on him, and their shadowy figures were now bearing down on him.

Hopping up onto a grassy bank, he dropped down through a hedge into the farmyard. He was half thinking that he might find refuge in the barn or one of the other outhouses, when he found himself face to face with a billy goat. It was, he realised, the same goat that had butted him on the backside the last time he had visited the farm. The memory of that experience was still a very painful one, and with an agility that he never knew he had, he side-stepped the goat before its great horned head could strike again.

The two dogs weren't so lucky. While most of the farm was theirs, to come and go in as they pleased, this corner of the yard belonged to the goat. Having missed one intruder, its head was lowered and ready for the next, and one by one, it sent them sailing through the air. Yelping in pain, the two dogs picked themselves up and limped away towards the farmhouse, all thoughts of foxes forgotten. Young Black Tip paused only long enough to make sure he wasn't being followed, then slipped back out of the farmyard and rejoined the others.

FOURTEEN

The Year of the Bee

Old Sage Brush had decided that his group should take the long way round. When Little Running Fox and Twinkle questioned the wisdom of this he just smiled and told them, 'Sometimes the longest way round is the shortest.' They nodded, and when he didn't explain, they thought about it, and when they thought about it they understood. If they ran into the giant hounds again, there was no knowing where they would end up. Some of them might even end up dead. For whatever about those who were young and fleet of foot, there was no way the old fox would be able to outrun the giant hounds again. And then there were the badgers. It had taken cunning to shake off the hounds the last time, and cunning was something badgers didn't appear to have.

Apart from their desire to find a new home, the badgers seemed to be interested only in eating and sleeping. Perhaps, the young foxes thought, it was life at the edge of the Fragrant Wood that had made them so easy-going. As they had said themselves, all they had to do when they wanted a change of food was to eat the blackberries that grew above them. Bramble was big, almost as big as Musta, and would probably have taken over the sett one day. However, according to Blackberry, his mate, that was a responsibility he didn't wish for. Nor did she. They had a very close relationship with their two cubs, and all they wanted do was set up a family unit of their own. Things had become too crowded on their island home, there were too many mouths to feed and food had become scarce.

Whether it was to make up for that time of scarcity, or because they were travelling so much, the young foxes didn't know; but Bramble and Blackberry were enjoying their food. It was a new experience for them when, on occasion, they had to forage for food during the day, but day or night, it didn't matter, and whenever they found themselves in the darkness of a sett they enjoyed the luxury of sleeping on a full stomach.

Food, on the other hand, didn't seem to improve the frailty of Old Sage Brush. He still enjoyed the rabbits, frogs and other morsels that the younger foxes brought him, but nothing could roll back the years. He tired easily and for this reason the other foxes came to welcome the eating and sleeping habits of the badgers. The frequent stops gave the old fox opportunities to rest, and gave the young some time to themselves.

'What if the other two groups arrive at the meeting place first?' wondered Twinkle, during one of these breaks.

Little Running Fox shrugged. 'I don't see that it makes any difference. They'll know the old fox has to take his time. They'll wait.'

They were lying in a patch of ferns at the edge of a small wood, which had provided an ideal resting place. Beneath a large boulder they had found a den that was warm and dry, and leaving the others to sleep, they had slipped outside. There was no sign of the wolfhounds, and as they lay in the sunshine and talked, the only other sound they could hear was the gurgling of a river beyond the trees.

'You know,' said Twinkle, 'I'd love to get Old Sage Brush something special to eat when he wakes up.'

'Like what?' asked Little Running Fox.

'I don't know . . .' Twinkle swivelled her large ears around so that she could take in more of the sounds from the river. 'Maybe a duck egg, or something like that'.

'And what about the badger cubs?'

Twinkle raised her head. The two cubs, she could see, had also slipped away and were playing nearby. 'We won't catch much if we have to take them with us,' she said. 'Anyway, they're always racing back and forth to their mother. They'll be all right.'

Little Running Fox got up. The badger cubs had begun a rough-and-tumble game of tag, and didn't even seem to be aware that they were there. 'Maybe,' she said, 'we could find two duck eggs.'

Twinkle, who was on her feet now too, smiled. 'Who ever heard of a duck that only laid two eggs?'

Quietly they stole away through the ferns, hopped over a ditch, and trotted through the wood towards the river. Beneath their paws the moss was soft and spongy, and had it not been for the carefree manner in which they moved, the birds in the trees above would not even have noted their passing.

'Do you think,' said Twinkle, 'we'll ever find the Fragrant Wood?'

'Of course we will,' her friend told her. 'Anyway, where else are we going to take the badgers? We can hardly bring them back to Beech Paw with us.'

'True,' said Twinkle. 'But you know what I mean.'

'You mean, will we find the Fragrant Wood before the wolfhounds find us?'

'I suppose so,' said Twinkle.

'Of course we will,' Little Running Fox assured her. 'Isn't that why we're taking the shortest way round?'

Twinkle smiled, saying, 'Very funny. But you're not to be making fun of Old Sage Brush. He's my grandfather, remember.'

'I know that,' said Little Running Fox. 'But do you think we'd be out looking for duck eggs if there was the slightest sign that the wolfhounds were around?'

Before Twinkle could reply, they heard the thudding of heavy paws behind them. Fearing that the giant hounds were bearing down on them, they turned around, ready to flee. To their great relief, they saw it was only the badger cubs, running towards them for all they were worth.

'Can we come with you?' panted one of the cubs as they skidded to a halt.

Little Running Fox was already shaking her head, when the other pleaded, 'Please, we won't be any trouble.'

Twinkle looked at Little Running Fox, saying, 'Maybe it would be simpler to let them come along.'

'How are we going to catch anything if they're with us?' asked Little Running Fox. 'We hunt, they forage, and they're very noisy.'

'All we're going to hunt is duck eggs,' said Twinkle.

Little Running Fox smiled. 'You're right,' she said, and before the badger cubs could express their delight, she warned them, 'But you must keep quiet and do as you're told.'

The cubs promised they would. 'And another thing,' said Little Running Fox, looking at the two small striped heads. 'Remind us, which of you is which?'

'Let me guess,' said Twinkle, before they could reply. 'You're the one we called Caterpillar. Isn't that right?'

The cub smiled and nodded eagerly, and Little Running Fox added, 'Because you're always stretching up to the leaves looking for caterpillars?' The cub nodded and smiled again, delighted that she remembered.

Twinkle turned to the other cub. 'And you're the one that's always digging for grubs. Isn't that right?'

The second cub was smiling and nodding now, and Little Running Fox said, 'So we called you Grub. All right, but remember, no romping around, no squealing and no scratching. If the wolfhounds hear us you know what will happen to you.'

The cubs lowered their striped heads and started to back away. 'Come on,' Twinkle assured them, 'you'll be all right.'

Still the cubs hesitated, and Grub said, 'Our parents always told us the best way to avoid danger is to walk in the shadows. That way, they said, you can see better.'

Little Running Fox looked at Twinkle and gave her a knowing smile. From the mouths of cubs, here was wisdom indeed, advice intended for those who lived in the dark and foraged at dusk, but also a timely reminder to Twinkle and herself to be more careful in the light of day. 'Your parents are very wise,' she told the cubs.

'And I think we should follow their advice,' added Twinkle.

With the responsibility of the cubs now thrust upon them, the young foxes no longer felt free to wander through the trees at will. Avoiding the sunshine, they stayed in the shade and used well-worn paths that ran through the bushes. Soon the sound of the river began to get louder, and emerging from a patch of scrub ash, they found themselves on the bank of the river.

If the eyes of the badger cubs were small, those of the young foxes were big, bigger perhaps than their bellies. As they made their way up along the river bank, they spotted a mallard duck on a nest on the far side. However, the current was fast-flowing, and they knew that even if they did get across, they might not be able to get the eggs back. Then they came upon a swan sitting in the rushes and all thoughts of trying to get across to the duck's nest were forgotten.

'Why bother with a duck egg,' whispered Twinkle, 'when we can get a swan's?'

Little Running Fox smiled. 'Wouldn't that be something for the old fox to get his tongue around?'

The problem was, the swan refused to move, and her hostile hissing forced them to beat a hasty retreat back into the trees. The badger cubs got such a fright that they reached the trees first, and were now looking out at the giant bird with nothing short of wonder, for they had never seen a swan before.

'If we do get one of her eggs,' said Twinkle, 'do you think we'll be able to get our mouths around it?'

'Don't worry,' said Little Running Fox, 'we'll get it back, even if we have to roll it! The problem is, how are we going to get her off the nest?'

'Won't she have to leave it when she wants to eat?' suggested Caterpillar.

Twinkle nodded. 'But that's her mate out there in the river. He'll probably take over.'

'And we can't wait all day,' said Little Running Fox. As they lapsed into silence, the little fox lowered her nose so that it was resting on her paws. The swan, she could see, was sitting high on the riverbank, her long neck turned back as she preened her feathers with her beak. If only they could get her to move! All they needed was a few seconds.

Raising her eyes, Little Running Fox noticed that the swan was sitting beneath the arching branches of a sycamore tree that grew at the edge of the wood. Furthermore, a bees' nest hung from one of the branches. Slowly she rose to her feet. The bees' nest, she could see, was directly above the swan.

'That's it,' she said. 'If I could loosen the bees' nest so that it falls on the swan's nest, the bees would force the swan to move. Then we could snatch one of her eggs *and* the honey.'

'That's a great idea,' said Twinkle. 'But do you not think it's too dangerous? I mean, if the bees go for you instead of the swan, you won't be able to eat honey or anything else for a long time.'

'And how are you going to climb up to it?' asked Caterpillar.

'I can climb like a cat,' Little Running Fox assured them. Then turning to Twinkle, she lowered her head, saying, 'Sorry, I know you don't like talking about cats.' Before Twinkle could reply, she was gone, and a few moments later only her tail was visible as she pulled herself up into the branches of the sycamore.

'Why don't you like talking about cats?' asked Grub when the tail had gone.

Twinkle shrugged. 'I suppose it's because I can't bear to think about them. You see, when I was a cub, cats raided our earth. I only survived because my mother grabbed me and ran. I was too young to remember it, but my mother used to tell me about it. Now, even the thought of cats sends a shiver up my back.'

'Sorry,' said Grub, but the subject was quickly forgotten when they saw Little Running Fox making her way out along the branch towards the bees' nest. Flicking her tail this way and that to balance herself, the little fox edged herself closer and closer to the bees' nest. There were, the others could see, three honeycombs hanging from the branch, and bees were coming and going in a steady stream as they supplied the combs with nectar to turn into honey. A few more unsteady steps, and Little Running Fox was there.

The bees were still too busy to notice her. Quickly lowering a front paw, she sank her claws into one of the combs and wrenched it free. Immediately a cloud of bees began swarming around her. As the comb fell she struggled to turn, but lost her footing and plunged after it.

The swan was still preening herself when the honeycomb hit her on the head and bounced into the river. With a loud squawk, she got up and flapped her huge wings defiantly, but almost immediately Little Running Fox came crashing down beside her. Protesting loudly, the swan flapped her wings again and skidded down into the water. To the surprise of those who watched, they saw that she had not been sitting on a nest at all. Far from hatching eggs, she had a clutch of fluffy grey cygnets which were snuggling into one another in the grass close by. Seeing their mother take to the water, the cygnets immediately scrambled to their feet. With a few awkward steps they hopped over the bank and a moment later were swimming gracefully away from the intruders.

Having got over her surprise, Twinkle was about to rush forward to see if her friend was all right, when out of the corner of her eye she saw the swan's mate coming across the surface of the water at frightening speed. Half flying, half running, its neck was outstretched and its intentions were clear. 'Run!' she barked. 'Run!'

Whether Little Running Fox was aware of the danger that was bearing down on her or not, she had already been stung into action – for on scrambling to her feet, she found herself being assailed from all directions by a swarm of angry bees. Taking to her heels, she raced for the wood and had just dived under the scrub when the male swan came crashing up against it. Fortunately, the swan didn't follow, but the bees did, and it wasn't until she was halfway through the wood that they finally gave up.

'Are you all right?' asked Twinkle, when they stopped to get their breath back.

Little Running Fox was curling her tongue around her upper lip, which was beginning to swell. 'I got stung,' she replied. 'But it'll be all right.'

Twinkle smiled. I told you it was too dangerous.'

Little Running Fox laughed. 'I know. But it was a good idea all the same, wasn't it?'

'Do you think that's what Old Sage Brush meant when he said you can't lick honey from a briar?' asked Twinkle.

Little Running Fox shook her head. 'I doubt it. But now we know you can't lick honey from a swan either!'

They laughed heartily together and got up to go.

By this time, the two badger cubs were digging and scraping at a mossy bank.

'Come on,' Twinkle told them, 'it's time to get back. You can eat later.'

Ignoring her, the cubs continued to dig. Suddenly wasps began to emerge from the bank, and as they buzzed angrily around them, the two foxes withdrew to a safe distance.

'What are you doing?' asked Little Running Fox.

'We're digging for honey,' replied Grub.

'You can't get honey from a wasps' nest,' she told them. 'It doesn't have any.'

'But this is badger honey,' Caterpillar shouted back.

Puzzled, Little Running Fox and Twinkle watched and waited. Now and then they flicked their ears and shook their heads to keep the wasps away, and when that didn't work, they skipped and jumped and swished their tails. Had man seen them he might have thought they had taken leave of their senses, such were the antics they had to perform to keep the wasps away. The badger cubs, on the other hand, were digging away, completely unconcerned about the wasps that buzzed about their heads. Their ears and eyes were so small the wasps couldn't find them, and so a short time later the cubs emerged from clouds of excavated soil, each carrying in his mouth a comb the size and colour of a very large mushroom.

Unlike the comb that Little Running Fox had broken from the branch of the sycamore tree, these combs did not drip with honey, yet the wasps were just as tenacious as the bees in pursuing the intruders, and their stings were no less powerful.

'Come on,' said Little Running Fox, who had suffered enough stings for one day. 'Let's get out of here.'

Twinkle needed no second bidding. Together they bounded off through the wood, leaving the badger cubs to follow. Holding on tightly to their combs, the cubs galloped after them. They in turn were followed by the wasps, but by the time they reached the hollow under the boulder, the wasps had all but given up.

As the cubs dropped the combs on the flattened soil in front of their parents, Twinkle told Old Sage Brush, 'We were hoping to bring you a swan's egg, and maybe some honey.'

'Unfortunately the eggs had hatched and the honey fell into the river,' added Little Running Fox. 'The cubs thought they could make up for it by digging out a wasps' nest. I tried to tell them you can't get honey from a wasps' nest, but they brought it anyway.'

'I'm glad they did,' said Blackberry, 'and so will you be when I show you what's inside it. Look.' She broke open one of the combs to reveal a mass of wasp larvae. 'It's what we call badger honey.'

'You see, there's nothing so nice as the grubs in a wasps' nest,' added Bramble, 'if you can get them.' So saying, he broke the other comb in two and pushed half of it under the nose of Old Sage Brush.

The others watched as the old fox took a mouthful of the wasps' comb. Slowly he munched it and savoured its contents, and almost as if he was reluctant to let the taste pass from his mouth, he finally allowed it to trickle down into his stomach. 'Now,' he said, licking his lips in a sign of great satisfaction, 'who did I hear saying you can't lick honey from a briar?'

The younger foxes laughed, and even though Little Running Fox's lip was swollen and sore, they both joined the cubs in munching what was left of the wasps' nest.

Badgers, they agreed, might not have much cunning, but they certainly had good taste.

FIFTEEN

The Year of the Bird

The early-morning mist that had come to the aid of Young Black Tip's group now enveloped Fang, Scat and the badgers they were leading. It was the same low mist and it curled around them in the same ghostly fashion as they snuggled into one another beneath a clump of brambles on the edge of a meadow. The tips of some of the arching stems had touched the ground and taken root. The stems were also intertwined and interwoven with long withered grass, thus providing an ideal hiding place for rabbits, generations of which had established runs or tunnels beneath them. The brambles were also used by passing foxes, the tunnels providing pathways on which they could come and go, and plenty of cover in between, where they could rest or lie up when they weren't out hunting. The mist now provided added protection for Fang and his group, but it wouldn't serve them as well as it had served their friends.

Like the trees after which they were named, Birch and Ash were strong and young, and their two cubs were the product of their first mating. The cubs were sturdy and had no problem keeping up with their parents, something Fang and Scat soon came to appreciate. As a family unit, the badgers stayed close together, accepted the directions of their fox friends without question and, when on the move, ran as quietly and as quickly as it was possible for badgers to do. At all times they kept their striped heads down and their spirits up and it was clear to the foxes that, whatever about the other badgers, Birch and Ash were determined to find the green hill where, in the words of Meles, things grew in abundance and the cuckoo was at rest.

The only thing that tended to deflect them from their path was Ratwiddle. For some reason known only to himself, he had decided to follow Fang's group. As was his nature, though, he was with it but not part of it, and with the wolfhounds still out there somewhere, the dangers of this were obvious. Furthermore, his erratic behaviour meant that Fang and Scat were soon chasing him all over the place in their efforts to keep him under control. Even to the badgers, whose sense of direction was anything but good, it soon became clear that Ratwiddle had become a cuckoo in their nest, using up valuable time and energy, but worst of all, deflecting them from their chosen path.

This posed a serious dilemma for Fang and Scat. Their natural instinct was to protect their own kind. Yet they had promised to guide the badgers to their new home. For a while, they managed to do both, but gradually Ratwiddle slipped from their grasp, just as his own mind seemed to slip from reality, and they knew that they must press on regardless of what dangers his wanderings might bring either to him or to them.

By travelling during the day, Birch and Ash were able to plot the course they should take. This they did by consulting other badgers along the way. Each sett knew the general direction they should take and advised them of the markers they should look out for on the next stage of their journey. These the foxes located without too much difficulty, and determined to stick to their chosen path, the group pressed on. The hedgerows were their pathways, the lush growth of summer their cover, and few, apart from the birds in the bushes or the rabbits in the headlands, noted their passing. Others, however, had noted Ratwiddle's less cautious journey through the fields.

Waking to find that a low mist was enveloping the clump of brambles where they had spent the night, the badgers trotted out to feed. To their delight they found frogs hopping across the meadow and slugs climbing the stems of the long wet grass.

Unusually for him, Fang was still curled up in his den. Having regaled Scat into the early hours with stories of vixens he had met and mated with, and others he had loved and left, the older fox was still asleep. By way of thanks, and hoping that perhaps he might some night experience such amorous adventures himself, Scat slipped out with the intention of bringing Fang a tasty morsel for breakfast, only to rush back with the news that the river was on fire.

'What?' asked Fang, who was not yet fully awake.

'The river,' panted Scat. 'It's on fire.'

Fang got up. 'How can it be on fire?'

'Come and see for yourself,' said Scat. So saying, he dashed back out to the meadow, and Fang had no option but to follow him.

'Look!' Scat exclaimed when Fang joined him on the river bank. 'The smoke is rising from the water.'

'That's not smoke,' Fang told him. 'That's the mist.'

Being a young fox, this was something Scat had not seen before. Nor, if the truth be known, was it something Fang had seen very often either. He was about to say so when a waterhen scuttled out from the far bank. Seeing that it was agitated, the two of them looked up from the water. The mist lay thickly in the hollow beyond the far bank and from it emerged, like ghosts from the past, the huge hairy faces of the two wolfhounds. With a flick of their tails, Fang and Scat turned and fled back into the meadow. Behind them they could hear the giant hounds plunging into the water as they took up the chase.

Having heard the commotion, the badgers were already on the move when the foxes caught up with them, and together they ran for their lives. For a while the low mist worked in their favour. Being so tall, the wolfhounds were above it and couldn't see them, but they could hear them, especially when the badgers went crashing through a hedge or a field of grain. By listening to these tell-tale sounds, and by watching for birds that were frightened into flight, the wolfhounds were able to gauge their approximate location and follow closely behind.

Realising that by fleeing in such a fashion, they were giving themselves away, Fang called a halt in the middle of a field of wheat. 'Now,' he whispered, 'keep down and be quiet.' Hardly daring to breathe, they listened as the hounds crashed through the wheat looking for them, but now there was nothing to tell the hounds where their quarry might be. Instead, the foxes knew from the sounds where their pursuers were, and even though they were tempted at times to make a run for it, they sat tight. Gradually the giant hounds moved away, and when Fang judged it safe to move, he led his group out of the wheat field.

The wolfhounds, however, hadn't given up so easily. They knew the foxes were in the wheat field and they were waiting for them. By this time the sun had burned the mist from the fields and the hounds could see for the first time that their quarry also included four badgers. With renewed vigour they galloped after them and were only denied a kill when the badgers followed the foxes down into a deep drain covered with briars. Skidding to a halt, the hounds paced up and down, watching and waiting for another opportunity to resume the chase. Wet from the mist and salivating from the exertion of running, their long tongues were now flopping out over their sharp teeth and dripping beards, a frightening sight for any creature that had the misfortune to look up at them.

Down in the drain, the foxes and badgers waited and wondered what to do. They could hear the measured padding of the huge feet as the hounds paced up and down, and the heavy, fast breathing from the great-toothed jaws that had reached out to grab them. When, eventually, these sounds died down, Scat crawled up under the briars to see what was happening. The hounds, he reported, were now lying down, their huge stomachs heaving as they waited for their next meal.

'What are we going to do?' whispered Ash. They were lying in a trickle of water at the bottom of the drain, and she was trying to comfort her cubs as best she could.

'We can't outrun them, that's for sure,' Scat told her.

Fang agreed. 'We must give them the slip. The question is, how?'

They're lying down now,' said Birch, 'which means they're not expecting us to make a move for some time. And they're probably tired. Why don't we make our way down to the end of this ditch and just slip away?'

'They'd hear us,' said Scat.

'Not if we went one at a time,' suggested Birch.

'And what about your cubs?' asked Fang.

'They'll be all right,' Ash assured him. 'They're scared, that's all – like the rest of us. But they won't let us down.'

'You know,' said Scat, 'it's so simple it just might work.'

Fang nodded, and addressing Scat, who was now lying beyond the badgers, said, 'All right, off you go. We'll follow you one at a time. And be careful.'

There wasn't much water in the drain, but its trickling was enough to conceal any sounds they made, and a short time later they stole up out of it where it entered a pipe beneath the gateway of a field. There was still no move from the wolfhounds, and hardly able to believe their good fortune, the group took off again. Running as fast as their legs would carry them, they didn't stop until they had put what they considered to be a safe distance between them and the hounds.

The sun was high now, and the place they chose to stop was a corner of a field where a farmer had dumped a load of soil. There, weeds of various kinds – the flowers of the fields, as the foxes called them – had sprung up in great abundance. In the middle of these, they lay down to rest and hoped that they had finally escaped from the creatures they knew they could not possibly outrun.

What they dreamed of as they dozed, no one knows, but it's safe to assume that the giant hounds were never far from their thoughts. Nor, indeed, were they very far away in reality, for what a badger or fox might consider a safe distance was only a short gallop for a wolfhound.

In the days when wolfhounds were used to chase deer, they were considered ideal hunters, for they seldom barked and therefore didn't frighten their quarry away. Now this same characteristic enabled them to enter, unnoticed, the field where Fang and his group were resting. It was only when the foxes heard the padding and the panting of the huge beasts close by that they became aware of their presence. Slowly the badgers awoke to the danger as well, and in frightened whispers they all wondered what to do.

Fang eased himself up and peered out through the weeds. The hounds, he told the others, were very close to them. They had no hope of slipping away from them this time, and even if they did it was unlikely they would get enough of a head start to outrun them. Furthermore, the hounds were now wandering in their direction, and being so tall, would almost certainly see them if they looked over into the weeds.

In his nervousness, Scat was nibbling one of the flowers when he realised it was what Old Sage Brush had called a white bluebell. Already a strong aroma of garlic was assailing his sensitive nose, and he was about to spit it out when he had an idea. There were, he could see, several clumps of the flowers around them. 'Quickly,' he whispered to the others. 'Eat the white bluebells.' The others looked at him as if he had taken leave of his senses. 'Quickly,' he urged them. 'Chew the white bluebells. The smell will kill our scent!'

Realising what Scat had in mind, the others began chewing the white flowers. Almost immediately a strong smell of garlic rose from the patch of weeds. Being dogs that hunted by sight, it's questionable whether the wolfhounds would have picked up the scent of either fox or badger. However, they would almost certainly have seen them, had they got close enough. Thanks to Scat, the closest they got was not close enough. Repulsed by the smell of garlic, which was as offensive to them as it was to the foxes, they lowered their heads, snorted to clear their nostrils, and wandered away.

'Now,' said Fang, when the hounds had left the field. 'Let's get out of here.'

Off they went once more, but Scat's ploy with the garlic had only given them a brief respite. Soon the wolfhounds were on their trail again. The group was beginning to tire now, and they kept to the ditches, hoping against hope to come across a sett or earth where they could take refuge. Although the badgers didn't complain, Fang and Scat could see that the cubs couldn't keep going much longer. Unless they found safety soon, the cubs would never see the Fragrant Wood.

The last thought in the minds of the foxes at this stage was Ratwiddle. Unknown to them, he had never been far away, and it was only when they dived into a badger sett that they spotted him. On looking back out, Fang saw that the wolfhounds, which had been close on their heels, had skidded to a halt. But beyond them, to his utter amazement, he could see Ratwiddle sitting in the middle of the field. Furthermore, Ratwiddle was looking up at the sky while he had a good scratch, and seemed completely unaware that the hounds were now turning their attention to him.

Fang barked a warning to his friend, and dived back into the sett to alert Scat. Although he was tired, Scat was galvanised into action, and followed Fang back up to the entrance. To their dismay, they saw that the hounds had galloped off in pursuit of Ratwiddle.

Telling the badgers to stay where they were, they crept back out of the sett and cautiously circled the area. They were anxious to help Ratwiddle, but conscious of the fact that they were now tired and could easily fall victim to the hounds themselves.

Using all the cover they could find, Fang and Scat scouted around until they spotted Ratwiddle careering through a crop of young barley. Running alongside him, they tried to guide him towards the badger sett, but when they reached a meadow he lay down in a clump of rushes and refused to go any further.

'You stay with him,' panted Scat. 'I'll try and draw them off.' So saying, he raced away, and a few moments later Fang and Ratwiddle heard the hounds go thundering after him.

Wondering what was going on, Fang sat tight. If Ratwiddle was aware of what was happening, he said nothing. But when, a short time later, Scat rejoined them, Ratwiddle shot out of the rushes and once more the hounds thundered past.

'You know,' said Fang, and a smile crept across his face, 'I think Harebell told Ratwiddle their secret.'

'What secret?' panted Scat.

'Remember, when we chased the hares? We couldn't catch them. No matter how hard we tried, they always outran us.'

Scat nodded. 'So?'

'We weren't chasing one hare. We were chasing several. Just like the wolfhounds are doing now.'

'You mean they were running in relays?' asked Scat.

'Exactly.' Fang looked up as Ratwiddle came crashing back in to them. 'And now it's my turn to go.'

Scat looked at Ratwiddle, but still Ratwiddle gave no indication that he knew what was going on, or that he had thrown them a lifeline.

'There's a house over there,' Fang told Scat when he returned. 'Near the river. And there's a net. I think man is trying to catch birds in it. See if you can lure the hounds into it.'

There was no time for questions, as the hounds were coming up on them again, so Scat took off. Beyond the house he came to a patch of reeds where man had erected the net. Ducking underneath, he stopped on the far side, hoping that the hounds would follow. However, the hounds were hunting by sight. Seeing the net, they swerved around it and continued the chase.

'It didn't work,' he panted when he rejoined the others. 'But they're slowing down. I think they're getting tired.'

Ratwiddle bounded off now, and seeing him head for the house, Fang said, 'Let's follow and see what we can do.'

'What do you have in mind?' asked Scat.

'Maybe,' said Fang, and he swerved to avoid another tussock of grass, 'maybe we could confuse them. Get them into the net that way.'

They were approaching the reeds when the chirping of birds brought them to a halt. A number of small birds, they could see, were fluttering wildly in the net, trying to free themselves. And looking up at them, with great curiosity, were the giant hounds. Ratwiddle had stopped a short distance beyond and was sitting back, scratching himself, apparently unconcerned about what was going on. But it was obvious that the hounds had lost interest in him. Strange as it might seem, they had eyes only for the birds that were flapping in the net.

Fascinated by this turn of events, Fang and Scat watched as a man, who had heard the commotion, walked up to the net and caught the two hounds by their collars. The foxes couldn't know it, but it wasn't the first time the hounds had strayed from the big house. The man, of course, was well aware of it, and he reckoned it wouldn't be the last time either. He looked at Ratwiddle, then at the birds, and smiled. The hounds, he knew, would chase anything that moved, as they had inherited the hunting instinct of their ancestors. But while they were still as big as their ancestors, the things they chased were too small, and they seldom if ever caught anything. In fact, they were no longer regarded as hunters, but as gentle giants, bred by some people, like those in the big house, as pets and for show. Responding to the man's touch, the two runaways went meekly with him to an outhouse. Later, he would return them to their owner, but first he had to put rings on the birds and release them.

Seeing the hounds locked safely in the outhouse, Fang and Scat left Ratwiddle to his own devices and returned to the badgers.

SIXTEEN

The Year of the Cat

Fortified by rest, the taste of what the cubs had called badger honey, and the thoughtfulness of their young in trying to sweeten their journey, Old Sage Brush, Bramble and Blackberry had resumed their travels with renewed strength. Twinkle led the way, and as always the two badger cubs stayed close to their parents. Unaware that the wolfhounds were now safely locked away, Little Running Fox, acting on instructions from the old fox, stayed at the back, ranging far and wide to make sure the giant hounds wouldn't come upon them without warning.

Now and then Bramble and Blackberry visited other badgers along the way, and the information they brought back began to suggest that the Valley of the Dragon was not far distant. Why the valley should have been given such a name, neither fox nor badger could imagine. Nor could the foxes imagine it providing a place of sanctuary. However, Bramble and Blackberry were happy that there they would find the Fragrant Wood, where, according to their wise ones, the cuckoo would be at rest and death would never find them.

Meanwhile, it seemed, the cuckoo was never far away and it appeared to take many forms, for as they continued on their journey they encountered many obstacles. More often than not the only way to overcome them was to go around them, and sometimes they got the feeling that something unknown was intent on deflecting them from their path. That was how it felt when they found that they had arrived in a corner created by the crossing of man's pathways. Already they had succeeded in getting safely across several of his pathways, but those had been narrow paths that wound through the countryside like rivers and carried few of his machines. The paths they had now come to were high and wide and carried many machines which went thundering past at frightening speed.

It was coming on to dusk, and while the others waited in a clump of gorse in a nearby field, Twinkle climbed the embankment to see how they might get across this particular pathway and continue their journey. Several hedgehogs, she could see, had failed to make it across and lay squashed to death, their spines having provided no protection against man's machines. These machines now had a brightness in their eyes which made their approach difficult to gauge, but what stunned her more than anything else was the eyes that flared up out of the darkness of the path each time the machines drew near. 'There are cats out there,' she reported to the others. 'I could see their eyes!'

'How many are there?' asked Blackberry.

Breathless after dashing back with the news, Twinkle panted, 'There are long lines of them, and they've taken up position in the middle of man's pathway.'

Realising that if what she said was true, they could be in more danger from the cats than from man, Old Sage Brush asked Little Running Fox to check it out, and a short time later she came back with the same story. 'The strange thing is,' she reported, 'they haven't moved. As Twinkle says, they're just staying in a straight line in the middle of the pathway.'

'It's very strange all right,' agreed the old fox. 'But tell me, did they smell of cat?'

Twinkle shook her head and looked at Little Running Fox, who said, 'I don't know. I mean, I don't think so. Why do you ask?'

'Because,' the old fox told them, 'to see with your eyes alone is not to see at all. You must use all your senses.'

The young foxes, and indeed the badgers, thought this was a strange remark, coming as it did from a fox who could not see. Yet the wisdom of it was obvious to all.

Turning to Twinkle, the old fox suggested, 'Why don't you have another look?'

Being aware of Twinkle's fear of cats, Little Running Fox sprang to her feet, saying, 'Let me do it.'

'No, it's all right,' said Twinkle. 'I'll go.'

'Why don't you both go?' said the old fox.

Bramble and Blackberry looked at the old fox, but if he knew something the rest of them didn't know, he didn't say. Instead, he drew his tail around so that it covered the tip of his nose and appeared to go to sleep.

Peeping up over the embankment again, Twinkle and Little Running Fox could see that the cats were still there. Every time one of man's machines thundered past, the eyes lit up as if, powerless to keep the intruders at bay, the cats could do nothing but glare at them. Yet the cats never moved, not even to step out of the way. Nor, now that the foxes noticed it, did they smell of cat. Encouraged by this and determined to overcome her fear, Twinkle told Little Running Fox to wait, and when the pathway was clear, she ventured out into the middle of it. The eyes were still there, she could see, but there was no sign of the cats. Instead, she discovered, the eyes were set in the pathway, and were now dull and lifeless. 'They're not cats at all,' she called to Little Running Fox in amazement. 'They're just eyes. Dead eyes.'

'Still,' whispered her friend, who was still peeping over the embankment, 'be careful.'

Twinkle was examining the eyes with great curiosity when one of man's machines came roaring up. It bore down on them with such speed that Little Running Fox didn't even have time to bark a warning. Immediately the cats' eyes came to life and Twinkle got such a fright that she nearly jumped out of her skin. Barely had she landed when the machine came thundering past, giving her an even greater fright. Without thinking where she was going she bolted across the pathway and, before she knew it, found herself on the other side.

'Are you all right?' barked Little Running Fox when the machine had gone.

Twinkle had tumbled down the embankment opposite, and picking herself up, replied, 'I'm fine. Tell Old Sage Brush they're not really cats, but the pathway is too dangerous to cross.'

Somehow, Little Running Fox had a feeling that the old fox already knew both of these things. 'He won't be very pleased if he hears you've nearly been killed,' she called back.

'Don't tell him then,' came the reply from the far side. 'Just tell him we'll keep on going until we find some way to meet up.'

Because of the proximity of man and his machines, the old fox now agreed that it might be safer to continue under cover of darkness. Calling out every now and then to make sure they were moving together, Twinkle trotted along one side of the pathway, the rest of the group along the other side, until they came to a river that flowed underneath. The water touched each side of the archway, and with no way to walk through, Old Sage Brush decided they would have to swim.

'But it's dark,' protested Little Running Fox. 'We won't see where we're going.'

'You forget,' said the old fox. 'For me it is always dark. But I can see where I'm going if I hold on to your tail.'

'And we are more accustomed to the dark than the daylight,' added Blackberry.

Little Running Fox nodded. She told Twinkle what they were going to do, and with the old fox holding firmly on to her tail, she eased herself into the water. The badgers followed, and short as their tails were, they did the same. A short time later they had rejoined Twinkle on the far side, and were racing through the fields to meet up with their friends.

The other two groups were already at the appointed meeting place when they arrived, and had taken cover on a small hill covered with hazel and scrub. The old fox and his group slipped in beside them, and there as they rested, they entertained one another with stories of their adventures. Hop-along's group told of how they had used the low mist and a goat to escape from man. Fang's group related how they had outwitted the giant hounds by eating white bluebells and running in relays, while the old fox's group recalled how they had stung the wasps for a taste of badger honey and looked the cats straight in the eye. Nothing, it seemed, was too small or too big to be overcome; and convinced, by what had been said by the wise ones of their kind, that dragons existed only in the minds of those who feared them, they set forth on what they hoped was the last stage of their journey to the Valley of the Dragon.

How or why the hares had communicated their secret to Ratwiddle, none of the others knew. But of all the stories that were told, that was the one that lingered longest in their minds. Somehow or other, they knew, it was related to the strange power that

Ratwiddle had, the same power that had kept him safe from the giant hounds and seemed to keep him safe from other dangers as he drifted around the countryside on his own. So much, indeed, did thoughts of his relationship with the hares occupy their thoughts, that they forgot about that other part of his mind – the part that had warned them of the dangers they might expect in the Valley of the Dragon.

Still travelling in separate groups, but not far apart, they gradually left the lush meadows behind them and not long afterwards found themselves in an area of low, gently-sloping mountains. The foothills, they could see, were shrouded in mist, and hoping that beneath the mist lay the valley they were seeking, they kept going.

They were picking their way down the side of a mountain when the younger foxes, who had been scouting ahead, called a halt. Things, they felt, were not right. Bringing the others forward, they showed them how something seemed to have chewed up the soil and spat it out again. Bushes had been uprooted as if some huge creature had been digging beneath them for grubs. Then there were the few stunted trees that had dared to grow in such a barren place. They had been snapped in half and splintered, as if by giant jaws.

'I think we must be in the Valley of the Dragon,' whispered Scat.

'It can't be,' said Birch. 'Where are the birds on the branches singing?'

'And the cuckoo on top of the green hill?' added Ash.

'No,' said a strange voice, 'you are not in the Valley of the Dragon, but you are on the edge of it and what you see is the work of such creatures.'

Turning around, they found that while they had been preoccupied with the landscape that lay before them, a little fox had emerged from the maze of muddy tussocks and was standing close by. She was, they noted, a thin, humpy-backed little fox, not much bigger than a cat.

'Who are you?' Fang asked her, more in surprise than anything else.

'My name is Flame,' the stranger replied.

'What are you doing here?' inquired Hop-along.

'I live here,' the little fox replied.

'And these creatures you spoke of?' said Scat. 'What sort of things are they?'

'Dragons, of course,' the little vixen told him. 'And you would do well to let them sleep.'

'How do we do that?' asked She-la. Like the others, she was listening to what the little fox was saying but wasn't really believing it.

'What better way for creatures to sleep, than on a full stomach?' said Flame. 'Perhaps if you could catch them some food – hares, rabbits, or even frogs. I will take the food to them, and then, when they are asleep, I will guide you safely down the mountain.'

'I don't believe there's any such creature,' Scat told her.

'Oh, but there is,' insisted Flame. 'What else but a dragon could churn up a mountainside like that, pull the bushes up by the roots and bite the trees in half?'

Unable to imagine anything else that might do such damage, the others turned to Old Sage Brush for guidance.

The old fox, of course, couldn't see what was before them. However, he could see it all in his mind's eye, just as he could see the size of the creatures the little fox was warning them about.

'What puzzles me,' he said, speaking to Flame for the first time, 'is how a dragon could be satisfied with a few rabbits and frogs.'

'Perhaps,' the little fox replied, 'they would be happier to fill their stomachs with foxes and badgers.' She turned to go, adding, 'Believe me, this is a place of great danger for you. When the colour of blood comes upon the mountain, man will take his sheep to safety and you will do well to heed what I have told you.'

When the little fox had gone, and none of them could tell precisely where she went, they retreated to a rocky outcrop over which hung a screen of briars, and under this they settled down to consider what they should do.

'I can't get the scent of any such creature,' Twinkle said. 'Any more than I could smell cats on man's pathway.'

'Are you saying they aren't there then?' asked Young Black Tip.

'I don't know,' Twinkle replied. 'But Old Sage Brush has said we cannot see with our eyes alone.'

'I could see the dragons in my mind,' said the old fox. 'But I could not smell them either. Perhaps that is where they are – in our minds – and nowhere else.'

'If it is only in our minds that they exist,' argued Hop-along, 'then how do you account for what they have done to the mountain?'

'Fang,' said the old fox. 'I don't hear you saying anything.'

Drawing the air in through his nose, Fang took a deep breath. 'I smell something all right, but it's not dragons.'

She-la looked at him in surprise. 'What then?'

'All I can smell,' Fang told her, 'is fox.'

* * *

When the other foxes had gone out to hunt, Old Sage Brush adjourned to a quiet corner of the overhanging rock so that he could consider the situation further with Fang and Hop-along.

'What's she like, this little vixen?' asked the old fox.

'She's a sorry sight,' Fang told him. 'She's very small and thin, and her back is humped, like a cat's.'

'I don't know how she survives up here,' said Hop-along.

'And her mind?' asked the old fox.

Fang shrugged. 'It appears to me she still has the mind of a fox.'

Old Sage Brush nodded, but said no more. Curling his tail around in his customary fashion to cover his nose, he dozed as he waited for the hunters to return.

The badgers, who had retired to the opposite corner of their rocky hiding place, were also considering the situation.

'If I had really thought there were creatures like that here,' Alder was saying, 'I would never have allowed us to leave the island.'

Hazel shuffled closer to indicate her support for her mate, saying, 'Who was to know? I mean, even Musta told us he had never seen a dragon.'

'Nevertheless,' said Bramble, 'it was a big step to take, and now we've put our families in danger.'

'We would have been failing in our duty to our cubs if we hadn't tried to find them a new home,' said Blackberry.

'And Meles told us it wouldn't be easy,' Ash reminded them. 'She said we must be strong.'

Birch fluffed himself out so as to impress his mate, and told her, 'One thing we are not lacking in is strength. But what can we do? How can we protect our cubs against a creature such as this?'

'What Meles was saying,' said Ash gently, but firmly, 'was that we should be strong in our resolve.' She looked at their cubs, who were now fast asleep, and added, 'Anyway, it's too late to turn back now.'

'Let's not panic,' Blackberry told them. 'On the way here, our fox friends have brought us through many dangers. Even when the situation seemed hopeless, they thought of something. Perhaps they can do the same again.'

If Old Sage Brush was listening to what the badgers were saying, he gave them no words of reassurance. If the truth be known, he was thinking not of dragons, or of badgers, but of a little fox called Flame, and when the younger foxes began to return with food, he said to Scat, 'Tell me, what's she like?'

'Who?' asked Scat, who had returned from the lower slopes with a rabbit.

'You know who,' said the old fox. 'The little one who warned us of the dragons.'

'Oh, her,' Scat replied. He was munching away now, and as he did so, he went on, 'She's lovely. She's small, like myself, and her eyes are big and round, like the wide eye of gloomglow. And she's very intelligent.'

Old Sage Brush grunted, saying, 'Mmm. I thought as much.'

They ate their fill, and when they had finished, the old fox turned to Scat again and said, 'It seems to me we have more food than we need. Why don't you take some and give it to your little friend? What did you say her name was?'

'Flame. You mean, for the dragons?'

'Of course not,' said the old fox. 'For herself.'

Scat picked up the remains of a rabbit, and was about to race off, when the old fox added, 'And tell her we've decided to press ahead. Dragons or no dragons.'

Scat dropped the rabbit for a moment. 'But do you think that's safe?'

'I cannot see any dragons,' the old fox told him. 'Therefore, they do not frighten me. And I cannot smell them, so I do not sense that they will do us any harm. Furthermore, I cannot hear them, so why should we be afraid?'

SEVENTEEN

The Year of the Dragon

Had the old fox seen man and his dogs taking their sheep down from the mountain that evening, even though it was the height of summer, he might have had second thoughts. However, he could not see them, and those who could didn't mention it. Nor did they see the splotches of red that fluttered from the hilltops as they continued down the mountain the following morning. It was only when the earth began to tremble and burst into flame that they knew they had made a mistake, and as they ran for cover they recalled Ratwiddle's final prediction. 'I see dragons spitting at the mountain,' he had told them, 'and I see flames running to the sky.'

Neither the old fox nor the badgers could see what was happening, but when they heard what sounded like thunder and felt the earth tremble beneath them, they knew they were in grave danger. The other foxes, of course, could see it all and were mesmerised by what they saw. Down in the meadows, great tongues of flame were leaping from the earth. The flames rose so high they seemed to run to the sky and they were followed by a noise like thunder that echoed through the valley. At the same time, long-necked creatures that were peeping out of a small wood began to breathe fire at them. Immediately, spittles of flame came shooting up at the mountain, whizzing over their heads, bouncing off the rocks and churning up the earth around them.

In blind panic, those who could see what was happening and those who couldn't scattered, seeking what cover they could find among the ruts and rocks of the mountain. But it was to no avail. Wherever they went they seemed to be in the path of the streaks of flame. Fang, who had been closest to Old Sage Brush, helped him as best he could, She-la helped Hop-along, and the young foxes helped the badgers, all hugging the earth as the burning blobs traced lines of fire in the sky above them.

Then, as they lay there and trembled and wondered what to do, they heard a familiar voice. 'This way,' it called to them. 'Over here'.

'It's Flame,' gasped Fang in the old fox's ear.

'Hurry,' barked the little mountain fox. 'This way.'

They needed no further bidding, and with one eye on the scorching sky above them, they dashed in twos and threes across to where they had seen the little fox.

Flame was already on the move and led them through a maze of humps and hollows where the rocks and other outcrops offered them most protection. A short time later, they were making their way down a small stream which, with the passage of time, had cut out a gully for itself on the side of the mountain. Only then, when they were out of sight, did the long-necked creatures cease to spit at them, and Flame allowed them to stop for a moment to get their breath. The badgers were huddled together now, comforting their young who were still trembling with fright. 'Have the dragons gone?' asked one of the cubs, but not knowing what was going on in the meadows, its elders were unable to give it much reassurance.

Old Sage Brush, however, was sniffing the air. 'It seems to me,' he said, 'I have smelled that scent before, and it wasn't the scent of a dragon.'

The other foxes were sniffing the air now too, and She-la agreed. 'Once,' she recalled, 'when I was in cub, I was wounded by a shooter, and that smell, that is the last thing I remembered.'

Cautiously Fang made his way up out of the rocky gully and peered down at the small wood. 'You're right,' he told the others. 'They're not dragons. They're shooters.'

Unknown to the foxes, man was now looking up towards them. The army officer who had ordered his soldiers to cease firing was scanning the mountainside through field glasses. Shortly after the practice shoot had started, he had spotted a movement up on the firing range. At first he thought it might have been a sheep. Yet he knew the farmers had been notified and had taken their sheep off the mountain the previous evening. Then he thought he saw a fox. Or was it a badger? He wasn't sure and so he had ordered his men to stop firing.

'Flame,' said the old fox, 'we owe you our thanks. But why did you come to our aid? After all, we gave you no food to feed the dragons.'

Flame smiled. 'Scat brought one rabbit, and that was enough for me.'

'But why did you not tell us they weren't really dragons?' asked Scat.

Flame shrugged her shoulders, which were so thin and puny they seemed to merge with her humpy back. 'Food doesn't come as easily to me as it does to others, and what better way to get rabbits and frogs than to let strangers catch them for me?'

'In return for safe passage across the mountain?' said Fang.

Flame nodded, and Old Sage Brush chuckled. 'Just as we thought. Yes, you may be small, but you are all fox.'

Using the gully as cover, Flame led them down the side of the mountain, and across into meadowland that was covered with gorse. Then, when they had split up into groups again, she took the first group through the fields to a grassy hill. There, in a small copse of evergreens that sheltered the stones of man's dead, they waited for the others.

With a degree of caution that would have been commended by Old Sage Brush, had he been able to see it, Flame used a different route to take the second group up to the hill. At Twinkle's suggestion, she had left Old Sage Brush and his group till last, so that the old fox could rest, and when she returned for them she was glad to see that they were ready to continue.

However, in varying her route to the hill for a third time, Flame encountered an unexpected problem.

They were just about to leave the meadows, when a rushy mound seemed to come to life a short distance ahead of them. Out of it rose a shooter – the strangest shooter they had ever seen. His face and clothes were the colour of the grass, twigs of alder seemed to be growing from his head and clumps of rushes sprouting from his body. Never before had they seen the like of him, except perhaps in the cornfields when farmers erected men of straw to frighten off the crows.

The man raised his gun, and the leading foxes bolted, taking the badgers with them to the safety of deeper cover. Unfortunately, Old Sage Brush couldn't see what was happening, and Twinkle, who as always was trotting along by his side, was so surprised she couldn't warn him. Seeing the man aiming his gun at them, she froze, transfixed by fear as she waited for him to fire. Yet it must be said that it wasn't fear for her own life that rooted her to the spot. It was fear of what was about to happen to the old fox. 'What brighter star to guide me than Twinkle?' he had said before their departure from the Land of Sinna. But instead of guiding him to safety she had allowed him to walk into danger. The man, she could see, was taking careful aim, and she was waiting for the shot when, to her surprise, he lowered his gun.

'Run!' she barked at the old fox. 'And keep close to me.'

Not realising what was happening, but sensing that danger was staring them in the face, the old fox turned as one with Twinkle, and running nose to tail, they followed the scent of the others up through the fields towards the small copse of evergreens on the grassy hill.

Unknown to Twinkle, the soldier had raised his gun, not to shoot, but to have a closer look at them through the telescopic sight. It was the first time he had seen a fox or a badger and the sight of several of them running through the rushes towards him had given him such a fright that he had scrambled to his feet. He assumed they were running from the sound of the big guns, and as the last two foxes ran up through the fields, he raised his rifle again to have another look at them. Later he would tell his friends that because he had been so well camouflaged, even the keen eyes of the foxes hadn't spotted him. But he wouldn't tell them that the animals had given him a fright.

'I told you they were in no danger,' Flame was assuring the others, but it was with enormous relief that both foxes and badgers welcomed Twinkle and Old Sage Brush back into their company.

They were now behind the shooters and when the firing resumed they watched in wonder as the rounds of tracer bullets leapt from the long-barrelled guns and hurtled up towards the mountain. Only then did the badgers question what they had heard their fox-friends saying.

'If it is man that is spitting fire at the mountain,' said Hazel, 'then why is it called the Valley of the Dragon?'

Flame smiled. 'It is your kind that call it the Valley of the Dragon, not us. I suppose – and I mean no offence – they could not see as far as we could.'

'But,' said Blackberry, 'our wise ones speak of this valley as a place where death will never find us. How can that be if it is full of shooters?'

'Strange as it may seem,' continued Flame, 'your wise ones were right. You see, these shooters only shoot at the mountain – never at us.'

'She's right,' said Twinkle. 'Otherwise, Old Sage Brush wouldn't be here now. Neither would I.'

'And those you would expect to shoot us never come,' Flame added. 'So you are safer here than anywhere else.'

'And the Fragrant Wood?' asked Ash.

'Later,' Flame told her. 'When you have rested and man has gone.'

When the firing died down, Old Sage Brush, Hop-along and She-la curled up among the roots of one of the evergreens and dozed. The badgers talked among themselves for some time, but eventually they curled up among the headstones and also fell asleep. Only the young foxes remained awake. Wide-eyed, they watched as the soldiers emerged from a long trench in the meadows, piled into their lorries and drove off. The guns that had spat like dragons and sent spittles of flame hurtling over their heads were towed away. The red warning flags were taken down and calm returned to the valley. Birds began to sing, and the badgers awoke to hear the soft sound of the cuckoo somewhere in the distance.

Turning to Flame, Caterpillar asked, 'Is the cuckoo at rest here?'

The little fox smiled at the young badger and told him, 'As much as anywhere else.'

The light was fading as Flame led them across the hills to a place where a shallow river was winding its way through the fields. Here and there alder trees clung to the crumbling banks, and in the pools beneath, the shadowy shapes of trout idled in the current. Not far above them, swallows skimmed the surface and streaked across meadows that were covered with buttercups. Beside the river lay a wood that was fringed with holly, mountain ash, and hazel. Some of the bushes were cloaked in honeysuckle, and what lay beyond the badgers could not see. But they could get the scent of woody odours which, to their long sensitive noses, were wondrously sweet, succulent and, above all, secret. And they knew without being told that they had arrived at the Fragrant Wood.

The adult badgers turned to the foxes, but before they could express the gratitude that was in their minds, another fox came careering across the field.

'Ratwiddle!' cried Scat. 'How did you get here?'

Not surprisingly, Ratwiddle ignored him, and with his head cocked to one side so that one eye was looking at the sky, he sat back and scratched himself.

Blackberry looked around at those who had helped them through one danger after another – a blind fox, one with three legs, one with a humpy back, and one whose mind was elsewhere. 'How can we thank you . . . ?' she began.

'There's no need,' said the old fox. 'The fact that you have found your new home is thanks enough.'

'Perhaps,' ventured Bramble, 'you too might find a new home here.'

She-la smiled. 'Our home is in the Land of Sinna.'

'And I, for one, have to get back,' said Young Black Tip. 'My mate and cubs are waiting for me.'

'I'll be on my way shortly too,' said Fang.

She-la looked at Hop-along, then at the old fox. The journey, she knew, had taken an awful lot out of them. 'Of course,' she said, 'the rest of us are in no real hurry.'

From somewhere deep in the wood, the harsh call of a cock pheasant came to their ears.

'You know,' said Hop-along, 'I think She-la's right. We are in no real hurry.'

Scat looked at Flame and smiled. He was in no hurry either, but he said nothing.

As the badgers waited to hear what the old fox had to say, the soft call of the cuckoo drifted across the countryside again.

'Perhaps,' said the old fox, 'we could stay until the cuckoo goes. After all, we wouldn't want it to divert us from our path!'

The badgers nodded their long striped heads in a gesture of appreciation, and turning away, scampered to the edge of the wood. There they savoured its secret scents once more and, with undisguised joy, plunged in under the bushes.

The foxes also found the scents of the wood greatly pleasing, and that night as they rested beneath it, She-la crept over to Old Sage Brush.

'Once,' she reminded him, 'when our young dogs were leaving the Land of Sinna, you told us the falling blossom never returns to the branch. Yet Scat returned.'

Old Sage Brush nodded. 'So he did.'

'Do you think he'll come back with us?' asked She-la.

The old fox rested his nose on his tail, and told her, 'You know, I think he might.' He smiled. 'And if he does, I think he'll bring another little blossom with him.'

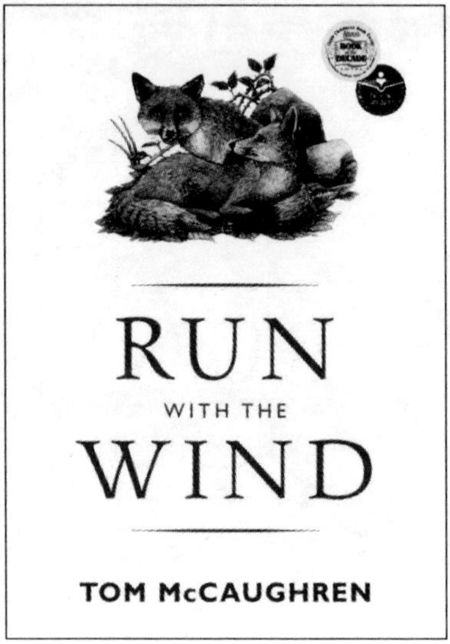

Book 1 – Run with the Wind
Tom McCaughren
RRP €6.99

Don't forget,' said the old fox, 'if danger threatens, run with the wind . . .'

In the Land of Sinna, Black Tip, Vickey, Old Sage Brush, Fang and the rest of the foxes who live around Beech Paw are in trouble. The fur companies are hunting them so much that the friends are beginning to think they are the last of their species. They have no choice but to set out in search of the secret of survival.

Join them in their exciting journey as they rediscover what it means to be 'as cunning as a fox'.

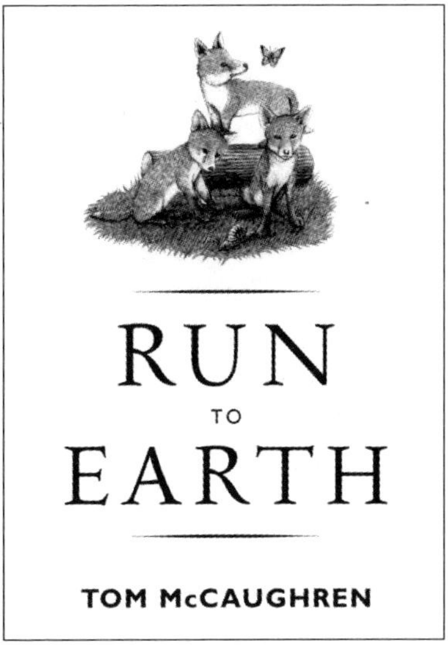

Book 2 – Run to Earth
Tom McCaughren
RRP €6.99

'Enemies we may be,' Fang told the badger, 'but if we don't work together we will lose to our greatest enemy – man.'

Free at last after their long and dangerous journey, Black Tip, Vickey and the other foxes are looking forward to cubbing time. But in the Land of Sinna the fight for survival never ends, and now a new threat hangs over the valley.

Moons of death strike from the evergreens and a powerful predator swoops from the sky. The new danger menaces all the animals in the valley, large and small. But, as natural enemies, will they come together to save the valley – and themselves?

Book 3 – Run Swift Run Free
Tom McCaughren
RRP €6.99

'Run Swift,' she whispered, and from the darkness beside her another voice added, 'run free . . .'

Summer has arrived and the fox cubs are growing up. Life is very exciting but it's also hard. The cubs have to learn the ways of the wild, how to stand up to other hunters and how to defeat their enemy, the trapper.

The final book in the award-winning trilogy, *Run with the Wind, Run to Earth* and *Run Swift, Run Free*, is a coming-of-age adventure as the young foxes learn to survive – but will they be able to fend for themselves and run swift, run free?

Book 4 – Run to the Ark
Tom McCaughren
RRP €6.99

'I knew when I saw the bow in the cloud,' Whiskers said, 'that I must be on my way again, leave all this filth that man has dumped in the rivers, and go to a place where he himself is but a leaf cast upon the water.'

The Ark appears above the Land of Sinna and the hard-pressed creatures of the valley see it as a sign. Whiskers tells his friends that somewhere beyond the Bow in the Sky lies a safe haven.

The three friends, badger, otter and fox, decide to brave a long and dangerous journey to find out. Along the way they meet a whole range of characters – Old Sage Brush, Vickey, Hop-along, She-la, Stumpy, Snout, Sniff and many others – but will they find the land beyond the Ark?

Book 6 – Run for Cover
Tom McCaughren
RRP €6.99

'Man can break an egg,' said Old Sage Brush, 'but he cannot put it back together again.'

The scientist in the land across the river had no idea what he was starting when he began experimenting with his gene machine. Now the Land of Sinna is being invaded by horrifying creatures – weeds big enough to eat a rabbit, a pig with two faces, a bird with two heads and a terrible predator, half-fox/half-cat, that is stalking the foxes.

When two fox cubs go missing Hop-along realises that it is up to him to lead Vickey, Black Tip, Skulking Dog, and the other foxes, on a quest to save them all.